D0787929

EMILY

DICKINSON

and Riddle

EMILY

DICKINSON

and Riddle

Dolores Dyer Lucas

NORTHERN ILLINOIS

UNIVERSITY

PRESS

Standard Book Number 87580–011–4

Library of Congress Card Number 73–76428

Copyright © 1969 by Northern Illinois University Press

DeKalb, Illinois 60115

CONTENTS

[v]

TO

JOHN J. GROSS
Bowling Green State University
AND
JOHN W. OSTROM
Wittenberg University

EMILY

DICKINSON

and Riddle

CHAPTER I

Introduction

PERHAPS THE NEAREST EMILY DICKINSON ever came to a definite statement about herself was "All men say 'What' to me, but I thought it a fashion—."[1] Characteristically, she was terse and equivocal. Yet when Charles R. Anderson threw down the gauntlet to the thoughtful Dickinson reader

> To give her poetry the serious attention it deserves. . . . to study it intensively, to stare a hole in the page until these apparently cryptic notations yield their full meaning . . .[2]

he, too, reaffirmed the essential character of her work —its apparently cryptic quality. What Emily Dick-

[1] Thomas H. Johnson and Theodora Ward, eds., *The Letters to Emily Dickinson*, 3 vols. (Cambridge: The Belknap Press of Harvard University Press, 1958), 2:271. Hereafter, citations to the letters will appear in the text by volume number and the number assigned to the letter as published in Johnson and Ward.

[2] Charles R. Anderson, *Emily Dickinson's Poetry: Stairway of Surprise* (New York: Holt, Rinehart & Winston, 1960), p. xiii.

[3]

inson wryly noted when she lived is still true: to say
"What?" is still in fashion.

From the publication of the first series of poems
in 1890, biographers and critics have asked
"What?" of the elusive Emily and her poetry. T. W.
Higginson set the stage in his Preface:

> I saw her but twice, face to face and brought
> away the impression of something as unique and
> remote as Undine or Mignon or Thekla.[3]

From impressions of her person, critics moved to
impressions of her poetry—equally equivocal:

> Her verses are like poetry pulled up by the roots,
> with rain, dew and earth still clinging, giving a
> freshness and fragrance not otherwise conveyed.[4]

or

> If she had mastered the rudiments of grammar
> and gone into metrical training for about fifteen
> years, she might have been an admirable lyric
> poet of the second magnitude. Pulling up roots is
> a very poor way to treat either flowers or poetry.[5]

After a brief respite of fifteen years (1900–1915)
Martha Dickinson Bianchi sounded the new keynote

[3] Thomas Wentworth Higginson, Preface to *Poems by
Emily Dickinson* (Boston: Roberts Brothers, 1890).

[4] *Ibid.*

[5] Thomas Bailey Aldrich, *The Atlantic Monthly*, 69
(January 1892), 143.

for subsequent endeavor: the psychic-wound approach. With variations sometimes more imaginative than illuminating, this emphasis culminated in Rebecca Patterson's *The Riddle of Emily Dickinson* (1951). Mrs. Patterson, in limiting herself to discovering the identity of the person about whom the poems were written, has not solved the riddle. Then, after Thomas H. Johnson's monumental variorum edition of all the poems and fragments (1955), more emphasis was rightly placed on the poetry. The result of the shifting emphasis, however, has been equally puzzling.

> This is her unique subject: the portrayals of *New Periods—of Pain*. And we need only look at the subject, and at the way she habitually structures it, to see that it conforms exactly to the preparation, the fact, the release, and the new preparation which are the basic stages of the menstrual cycle.[6]

Clearing the air of much of the controversy and providing valuable material for subsequent studies, Jay Leyda, adapting the approach which he had used in *The Melville Log*, reconstructed in *The Years and Hours of Emily Dickinson* (1960) Emily

---

[6] Clark Griffith, *The Long Shadow: Emily Dickinson's Tragic Poetry* (Princeton, N.J.: Princeton University Press, 1964), pp. 293–294.

[5]

Dickinson's life from all extant manuscripts and printed sources. This two-volume work, ordered only by chronology and without a comprehensive structure, is particularly fruitful for scholars. Significantly, such an approach has led Leyda to note that the riddle, or the deliberate omission of a circumstance too well known to need repeating, was a major device of both Emily Dickinson's letters and her poetry.[7]

Exciting new investigations into the poet's letters and literary sources are now underway. Her letters have, for example, been described as her conversation and autobiography conceived in much the same way as her poetry. And what was once generally regarded as true of her verse—that it contained little in the way of literary allusion—has recently been questioned. Jack L. Capps has presented convincing evidence that "an entire poem frequently turns upon an enigmatic allusion that becomes meaningful when related to her reading."[8]

From the welter of criticism, biography and critical biography, of which the preceding paragraphs are representative, a persistent problem emerges and a partial pattern is suggested. The two are related. A

[7] Jay Leyda, *The Years and Hours of Emily Dickinson*, 2 vols. (New Haven: Yale University Press, 1960), p. xxi.
[8] Jack L. Capps, *Emily Dickinson's Reading* (Cambridge: Harvard University Press, 1966), p. vii–viii.

statement of the problem is, at this point, relevant. Essentially it is this: biographical confusion and textual chaos have resulted in unfortunate critical evaluations. Regarding the biographical confusion, it is perhaps best to direct our attention to what is actually known: that something happened to Emily Dickinson during her late twenties and early thirties and that she did, indeed, become a poet. Beyond this, one is reminded of the poet's words, "biography convinces us of the fleeing of the biographied."

Textual confusion—resulting from the poet's failure to date her poems, her failure to indicate which versions were final drafts and which were not, as well as difficulties inherent in deciphering her idiosyncratic script and punctuation and early editings which "smoothed" her rhyme, diction and punctuation—has largely been overcome by Thomas Johnson's variorum edition of the poems which contain all known versions and fragments. But the extremely valuable variorum edition is not without limitation. It is, for example, impossible to determine the exact order of composition of these poems. Therefore, a chronology of the poems had to be based on extant copies of poems, on changes in handwriting and on age and types of paper used. Even the letters have suffered at the hands of censors and editors, notably in attempts to restore deleted portions of various letters. And evidence seems to indicate that the restoration process in some of the letters may simply have compounded original errors of deletion.[9]

Possibly because of the complex biographical-textual-critical problem surrounding this poet, the tendency has always been to emphasize a certain facet as, for example, the life as opposed to the poetry or, more recently, the letters as opposed to the life and poetry. Yet, precisely because of these several emphases which have evolved and because of proliferations now in process, a reconciliation of the life, letters and lyrics seems warranted.

What Allen Tate said so simply of Emily Dickinson in his perceptive essay still strikes essential truth: "There is none of whom it is truer to say that the poet *is* the poetry."

Yet in spite of a predilection on the part of both her apologists and critics for a favorite emphasis, all have united instinctively in noting the enigma of her life, or the ambiguity of her letters or a poetry verging perilously on riddle.[10] It is then the purpose of this study to offer the study and application of riddle as an approach to the life, letters and lyrics of Emily Dickinson.

[9] Johnson, ed., *The Letters of Emily Dickinson*, 1: xxv.
[10] Conrad Aiken, "Emily Dickinson" (first appeared in *The Dial*, April, 1924; next in the London *Bookman*, October, 1924, and the introductory essay from *Selected Poems of Emily Dickinson*, edited, with an Introduction, by Conrad Aiken (London: Jonathan Cape, 1924), pp. 5–22.

When we speak of "riddle" we find that we are dealing with something coeval with the human race, "the oldest extant form of humor and intellectual exercise,"[11] and also something found in the language of all civilized nations—a minor genre favored by such titans as Swift and Goethe. Then, too, attempts to prove on the basis of a common organizational pattern that oral or traditional riddles are the only true riddles have been unsuccessful.[12] Actually, all that is necessary to the structure of riddle is "one or more descriptive elements,"[13] and, for this reason, a riddle can be either prose or poetry, oral or written.

And although Emily Dickinson did not usually choose the prose form of the riddle—to have done so would probably have placed her firmly among the classics of children's literature where her detractors

[11] Robert Spiller et al., eds., Literary History of the United States, 3d ed. (New York: Macmillan, 1963), pp. 725–726.

[12] The pattern given by The Dictionary of World Literature (pp. 348–349) for a popular riddle is as follows: introductory element, consisting of a scene or summons; descriptive core, sometimes including a name; contradictory core, suggesting the act, object or aspect to be reconciled; and concluding element, summoning the reader to guess, offering a promise of reward or punishment. "Humpty-Dumpty," a well-known traditional riddle, lacks both introduction and conclusion.

[13] Robert A. Georges and Alan Dundes, "Toward a Structural Definition of the Riddle," Journal of American Folklore 76 (1963): 111–118.

[9]

have, incidentally, suggested she may belong—she was, upon occasion, quite capable of its use. In a letter to Emily Fowler (Ford), dated about 1851, we read:

> *Solve this little problem, dear Emily, if you possibly can: You have "so many" friends—you know how very many—then if all of them love you half so well as me, say—how much will it make?*
>
> I, 40

More often, however, Emily chose to write literary riddles in poetry of varying degrees of complexity. Sometimes her riddles may represent the object as speaking in the first person, or, as in the one which follows, they may develop one or more contradictory elements at the expense of descriptive detail.

> Who is the East?
> The Yellow Man
> Who may be Purple if He can
> That carries in the Sun.
>
> Who is the West?
> The Purple Man
> Who may be Yellow if He can
> That lets Him out again.
>
> *1032*[14]

[14] The numbers after each poem are those assigned to each poem in Thomas H. Johnson, *The Poems of Emily Dickinson*, 3 vols.

This poem, vaguely reminiscent of nursery rhyme, emphasizes the contradictory elements; the following poem, one of her finest, is by way of being a riddle, too, though admittedly more sophisticated.[15]

Further in Summer than the Birds
Pathetic from the Grass
A minor Nation celebrates
It's unobtrusive Mass.

No Ordinance be seen
So gradual the Grace
A pensive Custom it becomes
Enlarging Loneliness.

Antiquest felt at Noon
When August burning low
Arise this spectral Canticle
Repose to typify

Remit as yet no Grace
No Furrow on the Glow
Yet a Druidic Difference
Enhances Nature now

1068

A valuable treatment of literary riddle, applicable to much of Emily Dickinson's poetry, occurs in

[15] Charles R. Anderson prints the lost Vanderbilt version of P-*1068* in *Stairway of Surprise*, pp. 150–151. In this version the "minor nation" and the "answer" to the poem is revealed as "My cricket."

the introduction of Paull F. Baum's translation of *Anglo Saxon Riddles of the Exeter Book*. His is, perhaps, the clearest, most nearly precise discussion of the subject. He writes

> Riddles belong to that large family of expressions in which something is represented as something else . . . A resemblance is stated or implied . . . But in the riddle there is an element of calculated deception; the resemblance is submerged in deliberate ambiguity or obscurity.[16]

Baum analyzes the types of ambiguity which may be present in a riddle. Illustrating the riddler's desire simply to test the reader's mental agility, a riddle may be a good-natured exercise of intelligence. Conversely, indicating the riddler's desire for superiority or his special knowledge which the reader does not have, the riddle becomes a trial of wits; in short, a game. There is a third kind of ambiguity common both to the riddles of the *Exeter Book* and the poems of Emily Dickinson. It is what Baum terms "middle ground ambiguity"; that is, "the victim can retort that by the stated terms there can be more than one answer."

Consider again the poem just mentioned, "Fur-

[16] Paull F. Baum, trans., *Anglo-Saxon Riddles of the Exeter Book* (Durham, N.C.: Duke University Press, 1963), p. x.

ther in Summer than the Birds." Charles R. Anderson has solved the riddle concerning the poem's subject when he notes that the poet once inclosed it in a
letter and, for the occasion of the letter, entitled this
poem "My Cricket."[17] Yet, the poem has with credi-
bility been interpreted as "pre-Christian nature rite
whose meaning is lost in the dim past,"[18] or an aliena-
tion-between-man-and-nature poem[19] or a poem "con-
veying the peculiar fascination which the transition
period between summer and fall had for this super-
sensitive woman poet."[20] Any and all of these answers would seem to fit the terms stated. Some would
have it that this is, in essence, the measure of her
greatness: a conscious and controlled exploitation of
ambiguity.

Since great poetry is ultimately discussed in
terms of metaphor, it seems necessary to attempt
now, as Aristotle did long ago in the *Rhetoric*, to
make some useful distinctions between metaphor and
riddle. In order to make the distinctions I must intro-
duce a third element, the joke. According to the
Dictionary of World Literature the relationship between metaphor and joke illustrates the relationship

[17] Anderson, *Stairway of Surprise*, p. 171.
[18] *Ibid.*, p. 169.
[19] Yvor Winters, "Emily Dickinson and the Limits of
Judgment" from *In Defense of Reason*, 3d ed. (Denver:
Alan Swallow, 1947), pp. 283–299.
[20] René Rapin, "Dickinson's 'Further in Summer than
the Birds'," *The Explicator* (February, 1954): Item 24.

between poetry and humor.[21] I would add that the relationship between metaphor and joke at least suggests what the position of riddle should be in a linear arrangement of the three. A metaphor, however defined, seeks essentially to unite two ideas which had seemed distinct. Conversely, a joke seeks to break or sever what had seemed united. The former is congruous; the latter, incongruous. In a linear arrangement of the three, metaphor, riddle, and joke, riddle would hold the medial position. Deliberately obscure, having an element of conscious deception, a riddle never really unites, nor does it sever cleanly either. It is ambiguous, neither separating nor uniting, but transitional in nature. This is a point peculiarly applicable to Emily Dickinson.

While a major contention of this study is that Emily Dickinson consciously exploited the technique of riddle in much of her work, this certainly does not mean that she was incapable of projecting imaginative metaphors. Just as the traditional maker of riddles often created metaphorical riddles, so Emily Dickinson was capable of rather brilliant metaphorical riddles in her poetry.[22] The following poem is a type of metaphorical riddle.

[21] Joseph T. Shipley, ed., *Dictionary of World Literature* (Paterson, N.J.: Littlefield, Adams & Co., 1964), p. 268.

[22] Indicating the interrelationship between metaphor and riddle are three Nordic variants of a popular subject

After great pain, a formal feeling comes—
The Nerves sit ceremonious, like Tombs—
The stiff Heart questions was it He, that bore,
And Yesterday, or Centuries before?

The Feet, mechanical, go round—
Of Ground, or Air, or Ought—
A Wooden way
Regardless grown,
A Quartz contentment, like a stone—

This is the Hour of Lead—
Remembered, if outlived,
As Freezing persons, recollect the Snow—
First—Chill—then Stupor—then the letting
    go—

341

---

of riddles—the rainbow. What is intriguing about these
variants is, first, they are atypical (a rainbow riddle usually
uses "bridge" as the metaphor for "rainbow") and, second,
they recall a line from a Dickinson poem, "As Children, to
the Rainbow's scarf," *496*. The following Nordic riddles,
suggesting Dickinson's "scarf" metaphor, are from *Myth:
A Symposium*, ed. Thomas A. Sebeok, p. 43.

What is that?
A towel sown with silk.
No one ever took it into his hands.

In the field a piece of silk in five colors.
Neither you nor I can grasp it.

On the sky there hangs a kerchief in red colors,
    so it is said.

[15]

After a first reading of this poem, one may notice that the metaphors seem to break down. The "stiff heart," a kind of metaphoric corpse, has a rudimentary consciousness ("it questions"). Actually, if the poem is describing a kind of living death, which seems to be the intent of the first line, then the metaphor is sound. The riddle is evident in the third stanza. The "Hour of Lead" or living death is compared to the "Remembered" process of freezing to death. One presumably cannot remember the process if one dies, and the use of the conditional "if out-lived" as a qualifying modifier of "Remembered" compounds the riddle further.

While a propensity for riddling is probably not characteristic of one section of our country more than another section, certain factors in the poet's background and in New England in general are offered as hypotheses for Emily Dickinson's use of the riddle. To begin with, the Bible, while not an ample source of riddles in itself, suggests an area in which riddles were often used, that is, to test children on their knowledge of its content. In addition to the religious interest in riddles, there has been, from earliest times, a legal interest in riddles concerned with family relationships.[23] Certainly, in a family of

[23] Archer Taylor, "Riddles Dealing with Family Relationships," *Journal of American Folklore* 51 (1938): 25–37.

lawyers, it is not inconceivable that Emily Dickinson may have become familiar with riddles from either or both of these sources. And of course there is the likelihood that she may have seen her first riddles in an early school book, but since it is now impossible to determine exactly which of the thousand books and manuscripts the poet or other members of her family read, this particular area seems fruitless for research.

Another practice of her age which certainly seems to have reinforced her use of riddles, or which at least indicates that they were popular in Amherst when she was young, was the sending of original valentines. The following valentine composed by Emily Dickinson and sent in February, 1851, to Elbridge G. Bowdoin seems to have accompanied a lamp-mat.

I *weave for the Lamp of* Evening—*but fairer colors than* mine *are twined while stars are shining.*

I *know of a shuttle swift—I know of a fairy gift —mat for the* "*Lamp of* Life"— *the little Bachelor's wife!*

I, *41*

What seems of much greater significance is that one riddle can actually be traced from her reading to her letters and finally into her poetry. Jay Leyda has recorded from the *New York Observer* of July 18, 1846, the following item:

[17]

(*Emily Dickinson memorizes or clips this poem.*)
The Life-Clock
Translated from the German
There is a little mystic clock,
   No human eye hath seen;
That beateth on—and beateth on,
   From morning until e'en . . . .[24]

The "life-clock" riddle appears in a letter written to Susan Gilbert, March 5, 1853.

Oh it has been so still, since when you went away, nothing but just the ticking of the two ceaseless clocks—swiftly the 'Little mystic one, no human eye hath seen,' but slowly and solemnly the tall clock upon the mantel—you remember that clock, Susie. It has the oddest way of striking twelve in the morning, and six in the afternoon, just as soon as you come.

                             i, *103*

The idea seems to have been one which appealed to her for here it is again, imaginatively transformed into a poem which is itself a kind of riddle. Notice that the ambiguity is two-fold; that is, the riddle can have more than one answer. The "Clock" which stopped can be a human life or more probably a human heart.

[24] Leyda, *The Years and Hours of Emily Dickinson,* 1:111.

A Clock stopped—
Not the Mantel's—
Geneva's farthest skill
Cant put the puppet bowing—
That just now dangled still—

. . .

Nods from the Gilded pointers—
Nods from the Seconds slim—
Decades of Arrogance between
The Dial life—
And Him—

287

And in her inimitable style and uncanny prose-
poetry, Emily Dickinson reveals her attitude about
riddle in a poem and in a prose comment to T. W.
Higginson.

The Riddle that we guess
We speedily despise—
Not anything is stale so long
As Yesterday's Surprise—

The Risks of Immortality are perhaps its' charm
—A secure Delight suffers in enchantment—
The larger Haunted House it seems, of maturer
Childhood—distant, an alarm—entered intimate at
last as a neighbor's Cottage—

II, *353*

The contents of this letter reveal the "essential oils" —to quote the poet—the audience, the subject and the speaker.

The speaker is a Child.

CHAPTER II

The Speaker

🌼 *I remember a tree in McLean Street, when you and we were a little girl, whose leaves went topsyturvy as often as a wind, and showed an ashen side— that's fright, that's Emily.*

II, 264

THE SPEAKER IS A CHILD. Indeed, a New England lady of the mid-nineteenth century might, in lieu of marriage, choose to be a teacher, a woman of letters, or a recluse, or she might choose the career of perpetual childhood. Emily Dickinson was well-suited for the last role. And in a letter written in 1862 to her Norcross cousins, the poet created an impression of herself, a view of the Child perhaps more significant than she realized. When Emily returned to an incident from childhood to describe her irrational "ashen" fears, she must certainly have had in mind the child's deprivation and sense of rejection

[21]

in a world of adults, its powerful but unchanneled demands on life, the frightened child's ambivalence toward home and the peculiar, but characteristic, child's-eye version of nature as a realm of pets and plants *and* a world of hostile, terrifying forces.

Given what Constance Rourke terms Emily Dickinson's natural "sense of scale" or the "small compass,"[1] her proclivity for the dramatic, even self-dramatic, childhood became for Dickinson an exciting resource for her life, her letters and her poetry. Still, the role of child did not simply provide much of the content and point of view of her art; rather, the child-role served the adult Emily Dickinson as a combination offense-defense mechanism by which she could endure a life rendered otherwise intolerable by her fears of God, nature and her own father. The subterfuge of childhood provided the illusion of innocence, as well as the anonymity and detachment associated with the playing of any part. And if this simple child ruse had its defensive uses, it could also serve as a rather effective weapon for frontal assaults: the role of the insignificant child provided the kind of freedom that Dickinson needed "to cope with —to castigate, or to put on trial, or to laugh up her sleeve at—a universe that is contaminated to the

[1] Constance Rourke, *American Humor: A Study of the National Character* (New York: Harcourt Brace & Co., 1931), p. 267.

core."[2] In short, the resources of childhood were the material for much of her art; the ruse of child was her method of survival in a sometimes hostile and alien world; and the role of child protected her from reprisal.

Like a child, Emily Dickinson loved games, whether they were played by lowering trays of gingerbread to wide-eyed children on the lawn below her bedroom, or games of "little-women," played in letters over the years with her Norcross cousins; or the game of hierarchies implicit in her poetry;[3] or even an occasional acrostic which could be utilized in a thank-you note. But when Emily Dickinson assumed one of the versions of Child, whether the sentimental, childish "Emilie" or that other child who must have her say and be safe from reprisal, she needed a special kind of game. She needed and employed the riddle. The manner in which Emily Dickinson used riddle as a child of her home and family, as a child of nature and as a child of the nineteenth century is worth observing.

The poet once wrote about her home that it was a "holy thing" and "nothing of doubt or distrust can

[2] Clark Griffith, *The Long Shadow: Emily Dickinson's Tragic Poetry* (Princeton, N.J.: Princeton University Press, 1964), p. 31.

[3] Richard Chase, *Emily Dickinson* (New York: William Sloane Assoc., 1951) p. 308.

enter its blessed portals" (i, 59). She was, however, not always able to maintain this view. Perhaps, of all her aphorisms for "home," the one most overlooked and most significant occurred in a letter to her cousin Frances Norcross. Emily wrote, "Home is the riddle of the wise—" (iii, 737). Whether she meant her immortal home, or the "house with cornice in the ground" or the "haunted house" of nature or even her own mind is uncertain. She could have meant all of these, or she may well have meant quite literally her own home in Amherst. In one of her most intriguing letters, written in 1851, she described a particular occasion on which the influence of her own home became a kind of riddle.

I put on my bonnet tonight, opened the gate very desperately, and for a little while, the suspense was terrible—I think I was held in check by some invisible agent, for I returned to the house without having done any harm!

i, *42*

Why, having rushed out of the house toward freedom, did she return like a child to its protection and seclusion? Though the actual cause of this action is not now known, the action itself is symbolic of the strong ambivalence which she felt and expressed toward her home. Having at least nominally made a bid for freedom, she was thwarted, "held in check"

and she returned to what she described in one riddle
as a "prison."

> How soft this Prison is
> How sweet these sullen bars
> No Despot but the King of Down
> Invented this repose
>
> Of Fate if this is All
> Has he no added Realm
> A Dungeon but a Kinsman is
> Incarceration—Home.
>
> *1334*

Conversely, the "prison" became a haven secured by
braving a perilous path best left in a child's night-
mare.

> Through lane it lay—thro' bramble—
> Through clearing and thro' wood—
> Banditti often passed us
> Upon the lonely road.
>
> The wolf came peering curious—
> The owl looked puzzled down—
> The serpent's satin figure
> Glid stealthily along—
>
> The tempests touched our garments—
> The lightning's poinards gleamed—
> Fierce from the Crag above us
> The hungry Vulture screamed—

[25]

The satyrs fingers beckoned—
The valley murmured "Come"—
These were the mates—
This was the road
These children fluttered home.

9

For the poet who regards her home as prison and refuge, the ambiguity of the riddle makes it the method of choice for the subject. Form and content are, in a sense, united.

But for Emily Dickinson, home encompassed more than an ambivalent attitude. It meant family— ties of blood and loyalty. Illustrative, perhaps, of the complexity of these relationships was Amy Lowell's abortive attempt to write a biography of Emily Dickinson based on her relationship to each member of the family. While an extensive analysis of Dickinson's relationship to each member of her family is not within the scope of this study, a cursory glance at the subject seems pertinent to a discussion of riddle.

Perhaps the real tragedy of Emily Dickinson's life was, after all, not so much her reclusive existence, unfortunate love affairs, or even the mediocrity of New England culture, but her persistent lifelong quest for an audience. Even Lavinia Dickinson, Emily's younger sister, noted the poet's constant search for the "rewarding person" with whom she could par=

begin another correspondence.[4] For a time that rewarding person seemed to be Susan Gilbert, who
became, through marriage to Austin, Susan Gilbert
Dickinson. But the differences in the two girls far
outweighed any imagined similarities; Susan Gilbert
lacked the kind of confidence generated by pedigree,
the stability inherent in an impeccable family name
such as "Dickinson." Although Susan Gilbert's intel-
lect and tastes were similar to the poet's, her inability
to reciprocate the kind of friendship that Emily
Dickinson demanded precipitated numerous rup-
tures and reconciliations between the two. Both,
however, shared in the cult of sentiment and renun-
ciation generated by the reading of D. G. Mitchell's
(Ik Marvell) novels; and then, too, Susan Gilbert
wrote poetry. Typical of the childlike pose that
Emily Dickinson adopted in her correspondence with
Susan Gilbert is the opening paragraph of a letter
written in March, 1853.

*I know dear Susie is busy, or she would not forget
her lone little Emilie . . . and the credulous little
heart, fond even tho' forsaken, will get it's big black*

par=[4] Millicent Todd Bingham, *Emily Dickinson's Home:
Letters of Edward Dickinson and His Family with Docu-
mentation and Comment* (New York: Harper & Brothers,
1955), p. 413.

par=

inkstand, and tell her once again how well it loves her.

ɪ, *103*

Significantly, "the credulous little heart" chose to immortalize Sue in a riddle poem.

> One Sister have I in our house,
> And one, a hedge away.
> There's only one recorded,
> But both belong to me.
>
> One came the road that I came—
> And wore my last year's gown—
> The other, as a bird her nest,
> Builded our hearts among.
>
> She did not sing as we did—
> It was a different tune—
> Herself to her a music
> As Bumble bee of June.[5]

14

Perhaps it was poetic truth or more probably Emily Dickinson had already, at the time of writing this

[5] This riddle is particularly fascinating because it indicates that there are, after all, certain connecting links between oral or traditional riddles and the literary variety. Both types can have as subject "family relationships." For a discussion of this theme in traditional riddles see Archer Taylor, "Riddles Dealing with Family Relationships," *Journal of American Folklore* 51 (1938): 25–37.

poem (1858), ruefully acknowledged that it was indeed "a different tune" that motivated "sister Sue."

Neither apparently was Austin Dickinson, the poet's brother, her audience. We must infer, from a letter written in June, 1851, that Austin had criticized Emily's oblique letter-writing style. Emily complained to Austin:

> *I feel quite like retiring, in presence of one so grand, and casting my small lot among small birds, and fishes—you say you dont comprehend me, you want a simpler style.* Gratitude *indeed for all my fine philosophy! I strove to be exalted thinking I might reach* you *and while I pant and struggle and climb the nearest cloud, you walk out very leisurely in your slippers from Empyrean, and without the* slightest *notice request me to get down! As* simple *as you please, the* simplest *sort of simple—I'll be a little ninny—a little pussy catty, a little Red Riding Hood.*
>
> I, *45*

Ingenious Emily had found the childish "little pussy catty" version of Child a strategic retreat when she realized that she had misjudged her brother's ability to comprehend the various puzzles she sent him in her letters. Her need for an audience was prodigious. In another letter to Austin written in the same month, she came very close to disobeying her own dictum by "telling all the truth." She closed her letter to Austin:

[29]

*If I had'nt been afraid that you would 'poke fun' at
my feelings, I had written a* sincere *letter, but since
the 'world is hollow, and Dollie is stuffed with saw-
dust,' I really do not think we had better expose our
feelings.*[6]

1, 42

Her quest for an audience must, at times, have
seemed hopeless.

But if, through lack of understanding, Austin
and Sue were not her audience, her father, through
his insensitive violations of the poet's privacy, became a kind of ominous audience. That this is true is
suggested in several of Emily Dickinson's letters to
her brother and clearly stated in one letter to Austin.

*I have telegraphed to Sue. Dont say anything about
it in the letter you write me next, for father reads all
your letters before he brings them home, and it might
make him feel unpleasantly.*

1, 106

The elder Dickinson's practice of reading his children's mail becomes important because it accounts
for much of the obscurity of her correspondence with
Austin and Sue. And it may account for some of the
idiosyncrasies of her poetry. Although a need for

[6] See Leyda, 1:201, for the cartoon which apparently
is the source of the "world is hollow" allusion.

privacy will not solve the riddle of the poem below, it does serve as a possible explanation for the poet's use of "it" and "they" for "you" and "he."

> My friend must be a Bird—
> Because it flies!
> Mortal, my friend must be,
> Because it dies!
> Barbs has it, like a Bee!
> Ah, curious friend!
> Thou puzzlest me![7]
>
> 92

Whatever the nature of the relationship between Emily and her father, he seems not to have been the stern "paterfamilias" as usually depicted. He did, in fact, allow Emily to develop the unusual pattern of her life with only an occasional admonition about her reading habits and her increasing absences from church services. In fact, Emily's father required only that she appear in public once each year as hostess of his commencement tea. There were, of course, the usual differences in attitudes on current problems, the usual abyss between two generations in the relationship between father and daughter. In one of the most humorous passages in all of the letters, Emily

[7] In *Portrait of Emily Dickinson*, David Higgins presents a convincing case that these ambiguities, first appearing in the 1859 packet of poems to "Master," are, in fact, designed for privacy (pp. 19–22).

Dickinson indicates the normal separation of two generations as well as her celebrated wit.

We had a very pleasant visit from the Monson folks —they came one noon and stayed till the next. They agree beautifully with Father on the 'present generation.' They decided that they hoped every young man who smoked would take fire. I respectfully intimated that I thought the result would be a vast conflagration, but was instantly put down.

I, *123*

Perhaps the most outstanding feature about the relationship between Emily Dickinson and her father was its very remoteness. Physical display of affection was studiously avoided. According to Lavinia Dickinson, Squire Dickinson "would rather have died than kissed them," and even Austin felt that only after his father's death could he kiss him as a parting gesture. In *The Lyman Letters* new light is shed on the enormous distance between Emily and her father, not in love and loyalty, but in simple understanding. The poet wrote:

My father seems to me often the oldest and the oddest sort of foreigner. Sometimes I say something and he stares in a curious sort of bewilderment though I speak a thought quite as old as his daughter.[8]

[8] Richard B. Sewall, ed., *The Lyman Letters: New Light on Emily Dickinson and Her Family* (Amherst: University of Massachusetts Press, 1965), p. 70.

Still, insofar as anyone could, she perceived the "intrinsic" worth of the man who had brought the railroad line to Amherst, who rang the church bells to alert the sleeping populace of Amherst that the Aurora Borealis had arrived, who carried a card marking his formal commitment to Calvinism in his forty-seventh year and who once beat a horse because it "didn't look quite umble."[9] The riddle of one of the finest fragments she ever wrote can be solved when we realize that it commemorates, in all probability, the death of her father.[10]

> Lay this Laurel on the One
> Too intrinsic for Renown—
> Laurel—vail your deathless tree—
> Him you chasten, that is He!
>
> *1393*

And the fact that a riddle should serve as a kind of dedication as it does in the Dickinson poem is not without ancient precedent.[11]

[9] Bingham, *Emily Dickinson's Home*, p. 235.

[10] Thomas H. Johnson, *Emily Dickinson: An Interpretive Biography* (Cambridge: Harvard University Press, 1955), p. 228.

[11] In *The Word Hoard* Margaret Williams records that "we find the great missionary bishop, Saint Boniface, sending back from the wilds of Germany a number of elaborate riddle-poems, serious, instructive, and complicated by the use of acrostics for the double purpose of solution and dedication to his friend, the Abbess Liofa," p. 135.

[33]

Another "house," besides the one in Amherst, in which Emily Dickinson was a restive inhabitant was the house of nature. Nature, for Emily Dickinson, was not only the well-known "haunted house" but also a "staunch Estate (*1077*)" or a "glad-gay" dwelling, "safe and sweet." Again, if one realizes that the speaker is a Child—to be sure, a precocious one—who has the kind of double vision which sees the world as an idyllic garden *and* a "maelstrom, with a notch," such widely divergent attitudes become understandable. Her mature poetry does indeed suggest both "Christopher Robin"[12] and the "Post-Romantic Child."[13] Riddle again becomes an important technique for both types of nature poetry.

Illustrative of the Christopher Robin view of nature and the use of riddle as a means of broadening the imaginative scope of the subject are the following poems:

> His Bill an Auger is
> His Head, a Cap and Frill
> He laboreth at every Tree
> A Worm, His utmost Goal.
> *1034*
> Pink—small—and punctual—
> Aromatic—low—
> Covert—in April—

[12] Chase, *Emily Dickinson*, p. 111.
[13] Griffith, *The Long Shadow*, pp. 37–38.

Candid—in May—
Dear to the Moss—
Known to the Knoll—
Next to the Robin
In every human Soul—
Bold little Beauty
Bedecked with thee
Nature forswears
Antiquity—[14]

1332

Of another order of riddle is the following poem:

A Visitor in Marl—
Who influences Flowers—
Till they are orderly as Busts—
And Elegant—as Glass—

Who visits in the Night—
And just before the Sun—
Concludes his glistening interview—
Caresses—and is gone—

But whom his fingers touched—
And where his feet have run—
And whatsoever Mouth he kissed—
Is as it had not been—

391

[14] The answers to *1034* and *1332* are "woodpecker" and "arbutus," respectively.

[35]

The portrait in miniature is present here and something of the sentimental association of nature with a human lover. But an interview with frost (symbolically death) leaves the Post-Romantic Child disillusioned between surfaces which glisten and reality which destroys. The deliberate ambiguity of the riddle becomes a perfect instrument for the poet to express her own double-view of nature and to give it a concrete form.

Another of Emily Dickinson's nature riddles is particularly interesting because of its associations with an Emerson poem.

> It sifts from Leaden Sieves—
> It powders all the Wood—
> It fills with Alabaster Wool
> The wrinkles of the Road
>
> It scatters like the Birds—
> Condenses like a Flock—
> Like Juggler's Figures situates
> Upon a baseless Arc—
>
> It traverses yet halts—
> Dispenses as it stays—
> Then curls itself in Capricorn,
> Denying that it was—[15]

311

[15] Charles R. Anderson in *Stairway of Surprise* indicates the text used here as the version preferred by the poet (pp. 159–162).

Charles R. Anderson has pointed out that this poem
was probably influenced by Emerson's "Snowstorm."
One of Dickinson's variants for the next to last line
employs a "swan" image found in the Emerson poem
and one of her manuscript fragments contains a
passage directly quoted from the Emerson poem.
However, the differences are more striking than the
similarities and serve to illustrate Dickinson's relationship to Emerson. Whereas the Emerson poem
may, as Anderson reads it, show the "world-spirit
delighting to manifest itself in forms,"[16] her poem,
through the symbolic value of "Alabaster," may establish the death of the year or it may even encompass
the end of time through "Capricorn," the zodiac sign
for the winter solstice, when, in folklore, the sun
stands still. More likely the poet is having an entertaining intellectual exercise in the presentation of
both possibilities. Then, too, this particular poem is
very "Dickinsonian" in that it is complicated further
by whether she means the sun or snow in the final
four lines. At any rate, Clark Griffith's comment that
she did not abandon Emersonian principles but in-
verted them seems most perceptive.[17] Where Emerson held nature to be benevolent, deliberate, symbolically significant, Dickinson found nature deliberately
unpredictable, the benevolence transitory and the
symbols intensely ambiguous. Indicative of her

[16] *Ibid.*, p. 180.
[17] Griffith, *The Long Shadow*, p. 25.

[37]

range of attitudes about nature are the following
poems. In the first one the poet sees nature as a
benevolent force.

> Nature—the Gentlest Mother is,
> Impatient of no Child—
> The feeblest—or the waywardest—
> Her Admonition mild—
>
> *790*

But in the next poem she describes nature in terms
which almost parody Emerson. Where Emerson
would see nature as a symbol of a benevolent Spirit,
Dickinson sees the spider as a symbol of God, but her
symbol, the spider, is essentially destructive.

> If any strike me on the street
> I can return the Blow—
> If any take my property
> According to the Law
> The Statute is my Learned friend
> But what redress can be
> For an offense nor here nor there
> So not in Equity—
> That Larceny of time and mind
> The marrow of the Day
> By spider, or forbid it Lord
> That I should specify.
>
> *1167*

And in the final poem of this cluster Dickinson finds nature intensely ambiguous.

> But nature is a stranger yet;
> The ones that cite her most
> Have never passed her haunted house,
> Nor simplified her ghost.
>
> To pity those that know her not
> Is helped by the regret
> That those who know her, know her less
> The nearer her they get.
>
> *1400*

If, however, Dickinson differs from Emerson, in her Post-Romantic Child role, she, at least, belongs to a large community of American writers who have, in varying degrees, been restless in that "monstrous house" of "Nature—the gentlest Mother."

Though Thoreau may have concluded that in a deeper sense nature was one and continuous, he spoke of the birth process as a separation and rending—as if "we had been thrust up through into nature like a wedge," and the death bell tolls occasionally even in Whitman.[18]

---

[18] Albert J. Gelpi, *Emily Dickinson: The Mind of the Poet* (Cambridge: Harvard University Press, 1965), pp. 4–5.

> Just as much for us that sobbing dirge of Na-
> ture,
> Just as much whence we come that blare of the
> cloud trumpets,
> We, capricious, brought hither we know not
> whence, spread out before you,
> You up there walking or sitting,
> Whoever you are, we too lie in drifts at your
> feet.[19]

Emily Dickinson, like Thoreau and Whitman, was ambivalent in her attitude toward nature. If she was not unnerved by dread of nature, still she could not always be sure and

> she was at times as lonely as Hawthorne's Good-
> man Brown in the heart's dark forest, as baffled
> as Melville by the whale's riddling blankness, as
> numb as Poe's Pym before the apocalyptic white
> cataract.[20]

Gelpi concludes that "the specter of extinction, which was the primal fear, could seem at times the only grace and final deliverance." And Emily Dickinson would have agreed.

[19] Walt Whitman, *Leaves of Grass* 2, 17, 6 in *The Complete Writings of Walt Whitman* (New York: G. P. Putnam's Sons, 1902), 10 volumes.

[20] Gelpi, *The Mind of the Poet*, pp. 35–36.

Many Things—are fruitless—
'Tis a Baffling Earth—
But there is no Gratitude
Like the Grace—of Death—
614

At this point we may observe that Gelpi's list of
American writers who both feared and favored extinction is incomplete without the one who was
"Youth" personified and paradoxically the most
death-ridden—Mark Twain. From *Pudd'nhead Wilson's Calendar* we read:

Whoever has lived long enough to find out what
life is, knows how deep a debt of gratitude we
owe to Adam, the first great benefactor of our
race. He brought death into the world.[21]

Child of the house in Amherst, child of nature,
Emily Dickinson was particularly a child of the nineteenth century. When we think of Emily Dickinson's
poetry in relation to her situation, we must think of it
as repudiating the mediocrity and slackness of her
society. If her society was lacking in institutional
and sacramental variety, she instituted in her verse a
private system of queenly estates. If the impetus of
her society was to level out emotion and intelligence

[21] Mark Twain, *Pudd'nhead Wilson* (The New American Library, Signet Edition: 1964), pp. 33–34.

into uniformity, the intent of her poetry was to affirm a universe in which dramatic distinctions existed between God, man and nature. Emily Dickinson early joined the ranks of American writers who have radically revolted against the spiritual slackness and uniformity about them. Of her culture she once wrote

> . . . Men die—externally—
> It is a truth—of Blood—
> But we—are dying in Drama—
> And Drama—is never dead—
>
> *531*

Nineteenth-century New England culture was indeed "dying in drama," in fact had from the very beginning been failing in its overemphasis on practical issues and unpoetized facts of pioneer experience. Governor William Bradford of Plymouth had set the stage.

> All sorts of roots and herbs in gardens grow,
> Parsnips, carrots, turnips, or what you'll sow,
> Onions, melons, cucumbers, radishes,
> Skirets, beets, coleworts, and fair cabbages.[22]

But an Emily Dickinson need not stand helplessly impotent on the margin of a society drifting now toward money, materialism and impersonality. If as

[22] George F. Whicher, *This Was a Poet* (New York: Charles Scribner's Sons, 1938), p. 158.

THE SPEAKER

Emerson had said, "Things are in the saddle," Dickinson's poems often demonstrate that the simplest commonplaces and most spectacular symbols of progress can be vitalized, and if one is audacious, even outrageously lampooned. The child can have her say and yet not fear reprisal. Her riddle of the railway train is illustrative.

> I like to see it lap the Miles—
> And lick the Valleys up—
> And stop to feed itself at Tanks—
> And then—prodigious step
>
> Around a Pile of Mountains—
> And supercilious peer
> In Shanties—by the sides of Roads—
> And then a Quarry pare
>
> To fit it's sides
> And crawl between
> Complaining all the while
> In horrid-hooting stanza—
> Then chase itself down Hill—
>
> And neigh like Boanerges—
> Then—prompter than a Star
> Stop—docile and omnipotent
> At it's own stable door—

585

[43]

In the chapter entitled "Sounds" in *Walden*, Thoreau offers a romanticized treatment of a railroad train as a "firesteed" of whom it "seems as if the earth had got a race now worthy to inhabit it."[23] Whitman also made a locomotive the subject of a poem ("To a Locomotive in Winter"), urging the Muse of poetry to "merge [the locomotive] in verse." Although Whitman's muse may not have chosen to accept the invitation, Dickinson's, we may infer, did. The Dickinson poem best illustrates Santayana's remark about the true poet who catches the charm of something or anything, dropping the thing itself. Again she had "dropped the thing itself," had utilized riddle to dramatize and even satirize the nineteenth-century symbol of material progress. "Drama —is never dead."[24]

If nineteenth-century New England was culturally languid, the writer's world—the "inner life"—

---

[23] For the Thoreauvian influences on this poem see Nathalia Wright, "Emily Dickinson's Boanerges and Thoreau's Atropos: Locomotives on the Same Line" *Modern Literature Notes* 72 (February, 1957): 101–103.

[24] These several references to the similarity of themes and sometimes even similarity of treatment of these themes certainly support R. W. B. Lewis' comment in the introduction to *The American Adam* about the "unconscious repetition" among American writers. However, in the case of Dickinson's locomotive riddle, the repetition does not make for "sheer dullness" as Lewis would have it. Her use of the riddle form prevents it.

was charged with the reverberations of a lifelong, death-long struggle between theology and evolution, between what might be called "the house that Darwin built" and "the house of the Lord." Although Emily Dickinson's knowledge of Darwin is an area not well understood, we may theorize that she was at least superficially aware of his work, if only through her family's close contact with the college. At any rate Darwin apparently could not fill the void of traditional Calvinism for Emily Dickinson for she, like a later poet—Stephen Crane, reacted to Darwinian thought, to natural selection simply as grist for the mill of her imaginative art. In the following little poem it is difficult to detect where the real center of irony is—with Darwin or with Calvin.

> Papa above!
> Regard a Mouse
> O'erpowered by the Cat!
> Reserve within thy kingdom
> A " 'Mansion' " for the Rat!
>
> *61*

Probably it is nearer the truth to say that Darwin represented one of an infinite number of modes of perception capable of being imaginatively exploited by the poet.

What of the traditional Calvinism in which she was reared? Actually, by the time Emily Dickinson was born (1830) Calvinism lacked the heroic proportion and tragic mode of early Puritanism. It could no longer hold together all of human experience in a comprehensible whole. The new order, as Allen Tate has remarked,

> tended to flatten it out in a common experience that was not quite in common; it exalted more and more the personal and the unique in the interior sense. Where the old-fashioned puritans got together on a rigid doctrine, and thus could be individualists in manners, the nineteenth-century New Englander, lacking a genuine religious center, began to be a social conformist . . . A great idea was breaking up, and society was moving toward external uniformity, which is usually the measure of the spiritual sterility inside.[25]

What Emily Dickinson was able to salvage from the wreckage of the "great idea" was the conception of it on the theological plane—without the commitment to it. Like a child's scuttling of accepted standards of a so-called rational world is Dickinson's comparison of the doctrine of the Unity of God and Christ to an irrational version of the "Courtship of Miles Standish." The one, she would point out, is no more absurd than the other.

[25] Allen Tate, "Emily Dickinson," *The Symposium* 3 (April, 1932): 206–26.

God is a distant—stately Lover—
Woos, as He states us—by His Son—
Verily, a Vicarious Courtship—
"Miles", and "Priscilla" were such an One—

But, lest the soul—like fair "Priscilla"
Choose the Envoy—and spurn the Groom—
Vouches, with hyperbolic archness—
"Miles", and "John Alden" were Synonym—

357

Dickinson, like many of her contemporaries, was trying to penetrate the riddle of God with the tools of orthodox definition which no longer satisfied. The dilemma of Samuel Bowles, a friend of the Dickinson family, was in part Emily Dickinson's dilemma. Bowles said that he "had great faith in man, and the faith in God is perfect, only it cannot describe and take hold of the object."[26] Emily knew the difficulty of taking hold of the object; that it could be achieved, if at all, only through humor or perhaps through riddle.

When Emily Dickinson said of her family that "They are religious . . . and address an Eclipse, every morning—whom they call their 'Father' " (ii, 261), she was expressing as well her own attitude

[26] George S. Merriam, *The Life and Times of Samuel Bowles*, vol. 1 (New York: Century, 1885), p. 339.

toward God. An "eclipse" is after all not a void but a darkened reality, and basically she conceived of God as a "Force illegible" (*820*); something easily seen but not easily understood, who might proceed by "inserting here—a Sun—/There—leaving out a Man—" (*724*).

When she was able to write of God in terms other than as a "Force," it was usually to personify Him as "Father," with herself cast in one of her many Child roles. In one of the most charming of these poems, a kind of riddle, she ponders the usefulness of man and perceives, in the analogy of angleworm and bird to man and God, an answer to the riddle. Significantly, her answer differs considerably from the Psalmist's, who first posed the question— "What is man that Thou art mindful of him?" She would seem to suggest that if man needs God, God must in some sense need man.

> Our little Kinsmen—after Rain
> In plenty may be seen,
> A Pink and Pulpy multitude
> The tepid Ground upon.
>
> A needless life, it seemed to me
> Until a little Bird
> As to a Hospitality
> Advanced and breakfasted.

As I of He, so God of Me
I pondered, may have judged,
And left the little Angle Worm
With Modesties enlarged.

885

As a child uncertain of her home and family,
uneasy in the great house of nature, unimpressed by
nineteenth-century progress and uncommitted to traditional Calvinism, Emily Dickinson, like the tree on
McClean street, "went topsy-turvy as often as a
wind." Understandably she had written "that's
fright, that's Emily." But what frightened her most
and what challenged her powers, mental and artistic,
to the utmost was Death, for "All but Death can be
Adjusted—(*794*)." Sometimes she could deal with
it coyly, even employing puns, as in the following
riddle

There's something quieter than sleep
Within this inner room!
It wears a sprig upon it's breast—
And will not tell it's name—

45

More often, however, her poetry was of a higher
order, but her theme that defied adjustment was always death.

[49]

CHAPTER III

The Subject

🌷 *That* Bareheaded life—*under the grass—worries one like a Wasp.*

II, *220*

THAT DEATH WAS THE MAJOR CONCERN of Emily Dickinson's life—that it was the subject of many of her letters, and was drawn into the texture of at least five hundred of the poems—is not a startling assertion. The poet's critics and biographers have frequently noted her predilection for this subject, as well as the remarkable language which enabled her —almost—to capture in imagery the "narrow loving," or the "White Exploit" or just the "Riddle" through which "one will walk today." Her first biographer, George F. Whicher, in *This Was a Poet*, established a trend when he noted that she recurred to death more frequently than to any other subject. And rightly recognizing that many poets have made death central to their poetry, Thomas Johnson was convinced that "Emily Dickinson did so in hers to an unusual degree." Charles R. Anderson also found in *Stairway of Surprise* that death and immortality were "the two profoundest themes that challenged her poetic powers"; while Thomas Ford indicates in a recent study that "The idea of death was for her the overwhelming, omnipresent emotional experience of her life, and powerfully influenced her poetry, especially in its intensity and richness."[1]

Biographers and critics have not erred in their assessments of the importance of death in the poet's life and art. She could hardly have avoided the funeral ritual for, when in her formative years she lived on Pleasant Street, every funeral procession in Amherst passed directly by her house. And if she turned away from the funeral cortege regularly passing below her window, she did not shun the statistics, found in newspapers and periodicals, which she avidly read. They informed her that

Brain fever, scarlet fever, typhoid fever, 'ulceration of the bowels' and dysentery were to be

[1] George F. Whicher, *This Was a Poet* (New York: Charles Scribner's Sons, 1938), p. 298; Thomas H. Johnson, *Emily Dickinson: An Interpretive Biography* (Cambridge: Harvard University Press, 1955), p. 203; Charles R. Anderson, *Emily Dickinson's Poetry: Stairway of Surprise* (New York: Holt, Rinehart & Winston, 1960), p. 284; Thomas W. Ford, *Heaven Beguiles the Tired* (University, Ala.: University of Alabama Press, 1966), p. 34.

[51]

expected in the summer. . . . Severe colds, developing into 'lung fever' and other 'pulmonary complaints,' took a heavy toll in Amherst throughout the winter. Little was known about preventive medicine. People died without warning, especially young people, of whom the majority succumbed to consumption.[2]

Statistics really only confirmed Emily Dickinson's expressions of concern which occur repeatedly in her profuse correspondence. And never did she express herself more succinctly nor more arrestingly than when she wrote "That Bareheaded Life—under the grass—worries one like a Wasp" (ii, 220). Yet when one reads, for example, the poet's letter to Abiah Root, written in March, 1846, one may miss the true significance of the event being described. The style of this letter seems heavily sentimental, almost as if a death which had occurred two years before the writing of the letter had been used simply as an occasion to develop a style in vogue.

She [Sophia Holland] was too lovely for earth, &
she was transplanted from earth to heaven. I visited
her often in sickness & watched over her bed. But at
length Reason fled and the physician forbid any but
the nurse to go into her room . . . At length the

[2] Millicent Todd Bingham, *Emily Dickinson's Home: Letters of Edward Dickinson and His Family* (New York: Harper & Bros., 1955), pp. 176–180.

doctor said she must die & allowed me to look at her
a moment through the open door. I took off my shoes
and stole softly to the sick room.

There she lay mild & beautiful as in health & her
pale features lit up with an unearthly-smile. I looked
as long as friends would permit & when they told me
I must look no longer I let them lead me away. I shed
no tear, for my heart was too full to weep, but after
she was laid in her coffin & I felt I could not call her
back again I gave way to a fixed melancholy.

I told no one the cause of my grief, though it was
gnawing at my very heart strings. I was not well &
I went to Boston & stayed a month & my health
improved so that my spirits were better.

I, *11*

Such an evaluation, that the poet has used the death
of a friend as an occasion to develop a writing style
which reminds one of Mark Twain's Emmeline
Grangerford, would be true but superficial. Emily
Dickinson had indeed kept the death watch and as a
result her parents had felt it necessary to send her to
visit relatives in Boston to recover from this event.

Sometimes Emily could, as she described it,
"sing, as the Boy does by the Burying Ground—because I am afraid" (II, 261). Because of her fears
and reservations and because she had found it best
not to reveal her true thoughts on any subject, she

could resort to jest. In a letter to Austin, written in March 1852, she wrote

> *'Mrs Skeeter' is very feeble, 'cant bear Allopathic treatment, cant have Homopathic'—dont want Hydropathic—Oh what a pickle she is in—should'nt think she would deign to live—it is so decidedly vulgar!*
>
> ɪ, 82

More often, however, the tone of the letters is not bravado but anguish. She wrote to a friend, Jane Humphrey, in 1852,

> *Dont mind what I say . . . but I think of the grave very often, and how much it has got of mine, and whether I can ever stop it from carrying off what I love.*
>
> ɪ, 86

Most poignant and most direct of all the letters dealing with death was the cry she uttered when her beloved young nephew Gilbert died.

> *'Open the Door, open the Door, they are waiting for me,' was Gilbert's sweet command in delirium. Who were waiting for him, all we possess we would give to know—Anguish at last opened it, and he ran to the little Grave at his Grandparents' feet—All this and more, though* is *there more? More than Love and Death? Then tell me it's name!*
>
> ɪɪɪ, 873

Actually she wrote both the letters and the poetry from a deep need to understand the nature of death in order to relieve her own doubts about the phenomenon. What will happen after death? What will death lead to? This was the absorbing problem of her life; it was, as Thomas Ford has declared, "not *a* riddle, but *the* riddle."[3]

At this point it seems desirable to offer some justification for ordering or unifying Dickinson's work around the theme of death, other than the fact that several critics have in the past established the precedent or because the death theme has always been a traditional theme for much of literature. A justification of such a concern is necessary because a cursory reading of the letters may lead one to believe that her emphasis on the subject was emotional and even morbid. Charles R. Anderson has noted with a great deal of perception that an "obsessive concern with it [death] is no more morbid than is a compulsion to escape from it. Attitudes toward death become valid when it is made the occasion of a search for meaning rather than expression of emotion for its own sake." Certainly, death is a valid subject for poetry in that it is the focal point of religion, raising questions of immortality and the point of measurement for humanists, too, who try to evaluate mortal life which is limited in its duration.[4]

While most biographers and critics have concurred with the poet that death was indeed central to

[3] Ford, *Heaven Beguiles the Tired*, p. 76.
[4] Anderson, *Stairway of Surprise*, p. 228.

her life and art, they have generally failed to see the significance to her art of such statements as that which she made in the letter to Jane Humphrey. The artistic equivalent of whether or not she could stop death from carrying off those whom she loved was, of course, whether or not she could somehow embody the subject itself in her art. It is indeed as Anderson has indicated, "a search for meaning," and given the nature of the subject—death—the search takes on the character of a quest.

One realizes anew that not only was death the ordeal of her personal life, testing alike a tentative, traditional faith and a tenuous hold on reality; but also that death was the supreme challenge to her poetic art, testing her ability, if not to solve the "Riddle of those who resting rise," at least to develop the "undeveloped freight," the mystery of death, by embodying it in its essential form.

Indeed, the eminent scholar H. M. Chadwick in his monumental *The Growth of Literature*, has discussed rather extensively the nature, development and use of riddles in various cultures at different stages of their evolution. And in his discussion Chadwick emphasizes the point that

> The asking and answering of riddle is traditionally regarded as an ordeal applied to people of intellectual pretensions as a test of culture in general, and of proficiency in natural science and the language of poetry in particular, though in

modern times it has come to be largely a matter of social entertainment.[5]

In the light of Chadwick's discussion, Dickinson's choice of riddle appears almost inevitable. Emily seems instinctively to have returned to the earliest usages of the riddle, to the ordeal and to the language of poetry because death was for her personally and artistically, as well as through the heritage of the Puritan culture, the severest test of life. And although her death riddles are not usually "modern" in the sense of being sources for social entertainment, they are sometimes capable merely of testing the agility of readers with intellectual pretensions. Of such an order are the following death riddles:

> All overgrown by cunning moss,
> All interspersed with weed,
> The little cage of "Currer Bell"
> In quiet "Haworth" laid.
>
> *148*
>
> Trudging to Eden, looking backward,
> I met Somebody's little Boy
> Asked him his name—He lisped me "Trot-
> wood"—
> Lady, did He belong to thee?
>
> *1020*

[5] H. M. Chadwick, *The Growth of Literature*, 3 vols. (Cambridge, Eng. and New York: The Macmillan Co., 1940), 3:154.

[57]

Fortunately for her reputation as a poet, Dickinson did not often choose to write "entertaining" death riddles. Nor did she choose to force an ambiguity beyond fair play through a specialized knowledge which her audience could not be expected to possess. The following poem, however, comes perilously close to overstraining an ambiguity.

> Went up a year this evening!
> I recollect it well!
> Amid no bells nor bravoes
> The bystanders will tell!
> Cheerful—as to the village—
> Tranquil—as to repose—
> Chastened—as to the Chapel
> This humble Tourist rose!
> Did not talk of returning!
> Alluded to no time
> When, were the gales propitious—
> We might look for him!
> Was grateful for the Roses
> In life's diverse boquet—
> Talked softly of new species
> To pick another day;
> Beguiling thus the wonder
> The *wondrous* nearer drew—
> Hands bustled at the moorings—
> The crowd respectful grew—
> Ascended from our vision
> To Countenances new!

A Difference—A Daisy—
Is all the rest I knew!

93

One may well ask what the subject of the preceding poem is. Is this poem about a balloon ascension, the death of a person or a year, or perhaps a soul's ascension? Or is it an association of the anniversary of a death with a balloon ascension? The last conjecture is probably soundest since the only other poem in which she uses a balloon metaphor associates it with death (700) and since the elliptical opening lines can be expanded into "[the soul, balloon] Went up a year [ago] this evening." The riddle, as well as the private knowledge too personal or esoteric for most audiences, is in the closing lines, especially in whatever personal meanings the word "Daisy" held for her.

Neither good-natured exercises nor a trial of wits, the majority of Emily Dickinson's death riddles follow Baum's third classification of the forms of ambiguity of riddles; that is, "the victim can retort that by the stated terms there can be more than one answer." One would add that when the subject is intrinsically ambiguous and when the speaker is deliberately ambiguous, whether because of the child's mask, or an honest philosophical dualism, or a desire simply to hold an audience, there *must* be more than one answer. Some of Emily Dickinson's finest poems

[59]

are death riddles which probe the philosophical puzzle of *why* death is; or explore the physiological problem of *what* death is; or attempt to penetrate the psychological problem, *what it is like* to die.

For Dickinson the philosophical problem was the old dilemma between a Christian's faith in immortality and a child-of-the-nineteenth-century's doubt of it, compounded by two additional factors: the transcendental assumption of the unity of reality and soul, and the poet's inability to reconcile appearance and fact, the thing seen and the thing unseen.[6] Philosophically, the riddle of death was the apparent dichotomy between the spirit which soars and the flesh which stinks—"the riddle of those who resting, rise."

> Some things that fly there be—
> Birds—Hours—the Bumblebee—
> Of these no Elegy.

[6] Many critics have called attention to the poet's lack of formalized conceptions. Richard Chase, for example, has pointed out that in "Death is a Dialogue between/The Spirit and the Dust (*976*)" death is first a dialogue and then a term of the dialogue (p. 176). Although Emily Dickinson did not subscribe either to a particular philosophical system or to the formalization of conceptions associated with most "schools" of philosophy, she possessed the power to see things in their elemental terms and to make us think we see them directly. What she lacked in terms of philosophy, the ability to reconcile appearance and reality, became the impetus of her poetry.

Some things that stay there be—
Grief—Hills—Eternity—
Nor this behooveth me.

There are that resting, rise.
Can I expound the skies?
How still the Riddle lies!

89

The philosophical riddle of death could in another
setting involve elements of Puritanism and Transcendentalism.

Two Lengths has every Day—
It's absolute extent
And Area superior
By Hope or Horror lent—

Eternity will be
Velocity or Pause
At Fundamental Signals
From Fundamental Laws.

To die is not to go—
On Doom's consummate Chart
No Territory new is staked—
Remain thou as thou art.

1295

And a variant for the last two lines of the second
stanza "Precisely as the Candidate/Preliminary

was," serves to increase the complexity of the poem. We now have an odd blending: Puritanism and Transcendentalism. Eternity will be life (Velocity) or death (Pause) depending on whether or not the "Candidate" is among God's elect. But in the final stanza, "Man's 'own personal expanse' will determine whether he will continue to 'move' after death or whether he will 'stop.' The stanza also implies that the problem of dualism will be 'solved' in 'eternity'."[7]

A final poem illustrating the philosophical riddle or that odd "Fork in Being's Road (615)" is memorable for a motif common to other American writers. In this poem the persona can go into the grave, "the forest of the dead," or to the City of God with "Eternity's White Flag—Before/and God—at every Gate—." Either way the color is white and no matter how one looks at it, death is the "White Exploit." Whiteness for Dickinson, as for Melville and Poe, "expressed, or veiled, the final ambiguous mystery."[8]

If Dickinson's philosophical death riddles represent an unsuccessful attempt to reorient herself in the universe, her physiological riddles indicate a life-long search for the spirit in the body. But where she seems incapable of any cogent philosophical position, she can, by contrast, be as analytical as a medical examiner who "hopes to test the validity of a theory and submits himself first to the test, or watches a

[7] Ford, *Heaven Beguiles the Tired*, pp. 148–149.
[8] Gelpi, *The Mind of the Poet*, p. 115.

patient with alert sensibilities to detect the true symptoms and eliminate the false.[9]

Lest Emily's almost clinically exact depiction of the corpse, the grave, the funeral procession, and the deathwatch be thought a kind of reincarnation of Mark Twain's Emmeline Grangerford (and her necrophilic preoccupations), one should recall that the deathwatch, particularly, was an important part of nineteenth-century New England culture. Caroline Hogue's description captures the flavor of the practice.

Before the age of powerful anodynes death was met in full consciousness, and the way of meeting it tended to be stereotype. It was affected with a public interest and concern, and was witnessed by family and friends. They crowded the death chamber to await expectantly a burst of dying energy to bring on the grand act of passing. Commonly it began with the last-minute bequests, the wayward were called to repentance, the backslider to reform, gospel hymns were sung, and finally as climax the dying one gave witness in words to the Redeemer's presence in the room, how He hovered, transplendent in the upper air, with open arms outstretched to receive the departing soul. This was death's great moment.[10]

[9] Johnson, *Interpretive Biography*, p. 207.
[10] Caroline Hogue, "Dickinson's 'I Heard A Fly Buzz When I Died,'" *The Explicator* 20 (November, 1961): Item 26.

And at the crucial moment Emily Dickinson was there raptly attentive for some "sign" of the King in the room or of the soul which was to begin its lonely flight. In order to receive the sign, one needed to record the data with precision even when it seemed ambiguous. The following well-known poem details the deathwatch: the "willing" of keepsakes, the last onset of physical death and then at the crucial moment "There interposed a Fly."

> I heard a Fly buzz—when I died—
> The Stillness in the Room
> Was like the Stillness in the Air—
> Between the Heaves of Storm—
>
> The Eyes around—had wrung them dry—
> And Breaths were gathering firm
> For that last Onset—when the King
> Be witnessed—in the Room—
>
> I willed my Keepsakes—Signed away
> What portion of me be
> Assignable—and then it was
> There interposed a Fly—
>
> With Blue—uncertain stumbling Buzz—
> Between the light—and me—
> And then the Windows failed—and then
> I could not see to see—

465

The conventional interpretation of this poem, as Anderson reads it, is that the poet is offering "simply an ironic reversal of the conventional attitudes of her time."[11] The persona has squandered the final moments and words on distributing tokens of life rather than messages from the next world. Then she could no longer "see to see." But what is the significance of the Fly? What is its relation to the dying person? If the "Fly" is a blowfly, does it symbolize the processes of putrefaction, or is it the sign of the winged soul and that the "King/Be witnessed—in the Room"?[12] The mystery evoked by the one word "Blue" in the final stanza is enough to indicate that the physiological riddle of death may have more than one answer.

Without doubt, Emily Dickinson excelled at the clinical description of corpses; she was indeed mistress of mortuary detail—"the soldered mouth," "the

[11] Anderson, *Stairway of Surprise*, p. 232.

[12] While the influence of Sir Thomas Browne's *Religio Medici* on E. D.'s poetry has been well explored (see Margery McKay's unpublished thesis, "Amazing Sense," Swarthmore College, 1936, and H. E. Childs' article in *American Literature*, January, 1951), no one, to the best of my knowledge, has pointed out that within the body of the *Religio* is one of Browne's poems in which a "Flie" may well have influenced the Dickinson poem. Browne wrote

There will I sit like that industrious Flie,
Buzzing Thy praises, which shall never die,
Till Death abrupts them, and succeeding Glory
Bid me go on in a more lasting story.

adamantine fingers" and the "glazed eye." Paradoxically, some of her best poems dealing with the physiology of the corpse are ambiguous, even deliberately evasive. Perhaps this should not seem surprising when we remember that people of her time and culture were so intimately acquainted with death that the poet's real problem was to revitalize the language in order to express her ideas, not to make clinical analyses. One of her methods was the riddle, which by its nature demands a revitalization of language and commands the kind of intellectual audience which she always craved. The following poem, actually a riddle whose answer is "grave," is particularly interesting because it indicates that she could exploit a conventional "Gothic" atmosphere, deftly avoiding mortuary detail, and yet could indicate by a final question the tremendous sense of separation which the riddle of death held for her.

> What Inn is this
> Where for the night
> Peculiar Traveller comes?
> Who is the Landlord?
> Where the maids?
> Behold, what curious rooms!
> No ruddy fires on the hearth—
> No brimming Tankards flow—
> Necromancer! Landlord!
> Who are these below?

115

A final poem in this cluster is illustrative of her best physiological death poems. All that it requires to alert one that he is to guess what the poet is describing is the formulaic "What am I?" In fact, it is something of a shock that what this poem details is not so much the death of a child as it is the description of a dead child, a corpse.

> She lay as if at play
> Her life had leaped away—
> Intending to return—
> But not so soon—
>
> Her Merry Arms, half dropt—
> As if for lull of sport—
> An instant had forgot
> The Trick to start—
>
> Her dancing Eyes—ajar—
> As if their Owner were
> Still sparkling through
> For fun—at you—
>
> Her Morning at the door—
> Devising, I am sure—
> To force her sleep—
> So light—so deep—
>
> 369

If death was a philosophical and physiological riddle, it was also a riddle with important psycholog-

[67]

ical implications. Finding in neither philosophy nor anatomy the answer to the Riddle, she turned to another avenue of approach: What is it like to die?

Occasionally she did seem to achieve a kind of mystical vision of what death, in the abstract sense, was like.

> 'Tis Compound Vision—
> Light—enabling Light—
> The Finite—furnished
> With the Infinite—
> Convex—and Concave Witness—
> Back—toward Time—
> And forward—
> Toward the God of Him—
>
> *906*

However, the vision always failed and most of her poetry articulates, not the achievement, but the struggle to create the bridge, the "Compound Vision" between time and eternity.

According to Anderson's reading of the following poem, "she could even satirize her own attempt at an inside view of the moment of death as well as the orthodox belief about it."[13]

> Cautious—We jar each other—
> And either—open the eyes—
> Lest the Phantasm—prove the Mistake—
> And the livid Surprise

[13] Anderson, *Stairway of Surprise*, p. 233.

Cool us to Shafts of Granite—
With just an Age—and Name—
And perhaps a phrase in Egyptian—
It's prudenter—to dream—

531

Since she saw more clearly than most poets what could and could not be comprehended in language, she soon learned that there was an alternative to the imaginative construction of one's own death. She could begin with the abstract and move to the concrete; she could personify death and, by this alternative, she could perhaps gain some insight into its nature. She could certainly achieve something finer in her art than such imaginative constructions; she could transfix death at the point of striking. And it really was not crucial whether or not her personifications of Death were inconsistent and ambiguous, for, as Emily conceived him, Death was a

protean figure, part element of nature, part erlking, part Grendel, but mostly country squire; a suave, elusive, persuasive, insinuating character, but always a very genteel and attentive Amherst friend and suitor.[14]

Perhaps one of the finest poems in the English language is "Because I could not stop for Death" which is a kind of riddle. Is the personification of Death in

[14] Johnson, *Interpretive Biography*, p. 219.

this poem that of a genteel Amherst gentleman-caller
or something else?

> Because I could not stop for Death—
> He kindly stopped for me—
> The Carriage held but just Ourselves—
> And Immortality.
>
> We slowly drove—He knew no haste
> And I had put away
> My labor and my leisure too,
> For his Civility—
>
> We passed the School, where Children strove
> At Recess—in the Ring—
> We passed the Fields of Gazing Grain—
> We passed the Setting Sun—
>
> Or rather—He passed Us—
> The Dews drew quivering and chill—
> For only Gossamer, my Gown—
> My Tippet—only Tulle—
>
> We paused before a House that seemed
> A Swelling of the Ground—
> The Roof was scarcely visible—
> The Cornice—in the Ground—
>
> Since then—'tis Centuries—and yet
> Feels shorter than the Day

I first surmised the Horses Heads
Were toward Eternity—

712

At any rate, as Clark Griffith has remarked, ". . . it
is a thoroughly tricky poem which invites either of
two quite different readings. . . ."[15] Pointing out
that the reader's reaction to the poem depends on
how he interprets the narrative detail, Griffith attempts to "yoke together" the traditional reading of
the poem in which Death is a genteel Amherst gentleman-caller and Immortality is the chaperone with
a second reading in which Death is a seducer and
Immortality his cohort in crime.[16] Griffith's second
reading may indicate an incomplete analysis of narrative detail or a very subjective interpretation (the
gossamer gown and tippet of tulle in stanza four
show "vulnerability"). Yet, his instinct is correct; it
is a very tricky poem. The poet has deliberately left
unresolved which set of associations is more applicable to the poem and to her personification of death
precisely because she, herself, does not know.[17]

"Because I could not stop for Death" is a fine

[15] Griffith, *The Long Shadow*, p. 128.
[16] *Ibid.*, p. 132.
[17] There may even be a third set of associations applicable to the personification of Death in this poem. Charles
Anderson in *Stairway of Surprise* presents convincing evidence that Death is a surrogate leading the persona to marriage with God (p. 246).

[71]

poem for many reasons, not the least of which is because it is the epitome of a sophisticated literary riddle. While the poem may "yoke together" double or even triple Death personifications, it is an excellent literary riddle because it fuses the element of deliberate ambiguity with that of intrinsic ambiguity.

Although she could solve the artistic problem by embodying it in riddles of ambiguous personification, she could never really assuage the fear which lay behind the attempt first to imagine an inside view of death and then to embody the ambiguity in personification. She feared above all else the loss of identify, the separation of soul, the annihilation of consciousness. Again, this concern is not unique to Emily Dickinson for Dorothea Krook has pointed out that the chief intellectual concern of nineteenth-century thought was with the the concept of self-consciousness."[18] Indeed, in her speculations about consciousness, Emily Dickinson is similar to another American writer, Henry James. Both artists were concerned with the loss of identity after death and interested in preserving selfhood. Henry James could believe that "the quantity or quality of our practice of consciousness in this world may have

[18] Dorothea Krook, *The Ordeal of Consciousness in Henry James* (New York: Cambridge University Press, 1962), p. 411.

something to say to it." He believed that the development of self could be so rich here that it couldn't stop but—as he succinctly stated it—"I don't speak of putting off of one's self; I speak only—if one has a self worth sixpence—of the getting it back."[19]

Dickinson could talk with Austin about the extension of consciousness, could use "Costumeless Consciousness" as her shock image for immortality, but she could never be sure; and, like James, she would infinitely have preferred that "if one has a self worth sixpence to get it back again." Similar to James in *The Jolly Corner*, Dickinson could use a house image when she chose to write about the alter ego or consciousness.

> One need not be a Chamber—to be Haunted—
> One need not be a House—
> The Brain has Corridors—surpassing
> Material Place—
>
> Far safer, of a Midnight Meeting
> External Ghost
> Than it's interior Confronting—
> That Cooler Host.
>
> Far safer, through an Abbey gallop,
> The Stone's a'chase—

[19] F. O. Matthiessen, *The Major Phase* (New York: Oxford University Press, 1960), pp. 146–148.

Than Unarmed, one's a'self encounter—
In lonesome Place—

Ourself behind ourself, concealed—
Should startle most—
Assassin hid in our Apartment
Be Horror's least.

The Body—borrows a Revolver—
He bolts the Door—
O'erlooking a superior spectre—
Or More—

670

The "Single Hound," the "superior spectre" and the
"I" of the following poem seem all to be identity, the
alter-ego, or the separable soul.

Though I than He—may longer live
He longer must—than I—
For I have but the power to kill,
Without—the power to die—

754

And a child-poem shows just how apprehensive she
was of the possibility of separation.

We must die—by and by—
Clergymen say—
Tim—shall—if I—do—
I—too—if he—

How shall we arrange it—
Tim—was—so—shy?
Take us simultaneous—Lord—
I—"Tim"—and—Me!

196

A rather remarkable correspondence seems evident between the first poem of this group "One need not be a Chamber—to be Haunted/One need not be a House" (*670*) and a very old type of riddle which describes blood, heart or death in terms of the house, placing the subject within an object within another object within a third object. Archer Taylor sees a connection between this type of house riddle and the theme of the separable soul in that both use the device just mentioned.[20] And Dickinson's poem would seem to indicate the use of the same kind of pattern in a literary riddle since she uses a house image in the description of the latent content of identity ("ourself behind ourself concealed" and "superior spectre") which is behind the manifest content of identity, within the mind which is within the body.

Like the perception of death, her perception of time was ambiguous and a fear of time probably

[20] Archer O. Taylor, *English Riddles from Oral Tradition* (Berkeley: University of California Press, 1951), p. 491.

[75]

shaped her attitude toward death.[21] For Emily Dickinson both Time and Death meant change; and while the change wrought by time could mean loss of order and stability or even chaos, the change wrought by death seemed absolute and irreversible. It was for this reason that facing the riddle of death could sometimes be almost inviting. If one were confused by "the riddle of those who resting rise," repelled by the "otherness" of the corpse and appalled by the prospect of loss or change in essential identity after death, one could at least take consolation in the fact that this was the ultimate in change, the refuge from temporality, the escape out of time.

Artistically, for Emily Dickinson, facing the riddle of death meant not only transfixing death in an ambiguous personification but also rendering the moment of death. Having struggled to measure this moment by space, time, and movement, she discovered the perfect means in that invention which measures time by motion, a clock. Significantly, as has been established in the introduction of this study, she was aided in her discovery by the German riddle entitled "The Life-Clock" and was perhaps directly influenced by this riddle in the poem which begins "A Clock Stopped" (*287*). This poem is remarkable because it contains nearly all the best qualities of her remarkable death poetry.

[21] Griffith, *The Long Shadow*, p. 111.

There is, first of all, the riddle.

> A Clock stopped—
> Not the Mantel's—

A human heart, which in its pulsations measures time not unlike the swinging pendulum, is the "Clock" not of the mantel.

And since the poem really concerns the moment of death, the philosophical, physiological and psychological riddle is there, too. She wrote

> An Awe came on the Trinket!
> The Figures hunched, with pain—
> Then quivered out of Decimals—
> Into Degreeless Noon—

Apparently, she was still searching the face of the corpse for some glimpse of heaven; "Awe" is Dickinson's word for the belief that the dead catch a glimpse of heaven at the moment of passing. She wisely leaves unresolved the question of whether the stopped clock has seen God. In the same stanza the passage out of time into timelessness is termed "degreeless noon." Just as she once described her own flight to heaven as "when I go out of Time" so the soul of this clock passes out of the decimals of human time into "Degreeless Noon."[22]

In the last stanza of the poem, the final word "Him" is also the final riddle.

[22] Anderson, *Stairway of Surprise*, p. 236.

Nods from the Gilded pointers—
Nods from the Seconds slim—
Decades of Arrogance between
The Dial life—
And Him—

287

"Him" may refer either to God or to the soul which has escaped into timelessness. In this case the "Decades of Arrogance" defines the absoluteness of the distance in time between the soul and its former brief life. "Arrogance" is her inspired word for the separation which she feared most.

"Arrogance" also illustrates her greatest gift— the use of words—which is essential both to a riddler and to the death poet who is a riddler. If the impetus behind the philosophical, psychological and physiological death riddles is a fear of change, a separation, a breakdown in communication, one need not wonder at the poet's fascination with the power of the individual word for communication. Could she work through language to reconcile apparent incongruities present in the universe? Thomas Ford has said that "if she could join into a meaningful whole seemingly disparate words, then perhaps she could entertain the notion that an apparently disordered universe might in reality be intact, though she would not be admitted to the secret in this life."[23] Could she

[23] Ford, *Heaven Beguiles the Tired*, p. 184.

share with an audience her fascination with words as a means of sounding the meaning of death in order to bridge the gap between mortality and supra-consciousness? Just as she could use a language term to define death as the "Hyphen of the Sea," she could use the poet's traditional concept of the riddle of death as the literary technique best tailored to her conception of the subject and the word.

Whether an interest in words gave rise to writing riddles or a love of puzzles fostered an interest in words is unimportant. What is important is that Emily Dickinson possessed the three time-tested qualifications necessary to one who is to engage in the riddler's art: knowledge, observation and rhetorical skill.[24] Since her rhetorical skills and acute powers of observation are well known, one can turn from them to the most significant of Chadwick's qualifications—"knowledge." What kind of knowledge did she possess? Certainly not that of an inside view of death. What she did possess, more than most people, was an instinctual perception and concern for words and their ways. She was, as Donald Thackrey has noted with a great deal of perception, a poet who "approached the writing of poetry inductively—that is, through the combining of words to arrive at whatever conclusion the word pattern seemed to suggest,

[24] Chadwick, *The Growth of Literature*, 2:742.

rather than using words as subordinate instruments in expressing a total conception."[25] With a knowledge of words and of the riddle form she hoped to gain essentially a knowledge of her subject; for what she wrote, after all, were literary riddles and her exploitation of the word was a good deal more sophisticated than what is found in the oral tradition of riddles.

Her viewpoint on the vitality of language is in its relationship to one of the more sophisticated literary riddles of the *Exeter Book* enough to establish her position in the line of writers who chose to use this minor genre. Incorporated into one of Emily Dickinson's letters was the following verse:

> A word is dead
> When it is said,
> Some say.
> I say it just
> Begins to live
> That day.
>   *1212*

Speech does not kill the power of words by consuming the word-hoard; rather, words are dead only when they lie inert in a dictionary, or perhaps when

[25] Donald E. Thackrey, "The Communication of the Word," *Emily Dickinson's Approach to Poetry* (Lincoln, Neb.: University of Nebraska Studies, New Series, no. 13, 1954).

they are consumed by a book worm. Here is the Anglo-Saxon riddle.

> A moth ate words. To me it seemed
> a remarkable fate, when I learned of the marvel,
> that the worm had swallowed the speech of a
>   man,
> a thief in the night, a renowned saying
> and its place itself. Though he swallowed the
>   word
> the thieving stranger was no whit the wiser.
>
> *42 K-D 47*[26]

How was she to communicate the search for meaning and the power of the vehicle itself—the language—to an audience? Two methods occurred to her: the method of discovery of meaning, and the method of creation of meaning. Just as she turned to the oldest usage of the riddle as an ordeal, so she discovered the meanings of words by returning to their etymological meanings.[27]

The other method, the creation of meanings, if more difficult, was ideally suited to Dickinson's inductive vision of poetry. In fact it is interesting that the instinct of an early anonymous critic seems to

[26] Baum, trans., *Anglo-Saxon Riddles of the Exeter Book*, pp. 34–35.

[27] Margaret Schlauk, *The Gift of Language* (New York: Dover, 1955) p. 231. See also pp. 235–255 for other methods of language revitalization which apply to Dickinson.

have been sound in noting that "her words are often
hard to wrench into appositeness with her very clear
thought. . . ." However, she was not afflicted with
aphasia, as the critic seemed to think. She was following her well-known precept of indirection by
making familiar words in new combinations say new
things, or, as Ford has explained, she used the device
of "slightly dislocating the word from its dictionary
meaning to fit the context of her poem."[28] For example, in "Twas Crisis—All the length had passed—
/That dull—benumbing time"/ (*948*) the word
"length" as something which passes in time is an
unusual usage. The meaning is further enriched by
the connotations of boredom and of the unwinding of
the length of life.[29]

The letters and poems reveal that Emily Dickinson never abandoned her efforts in piercing the riddle of death, though at the end much of the intensity
and fascination had gone. She seems to have realized
that like Parsival and the Grail or Ahab and Moby
Dick she had embarked upon a hopeless quest.

> Finding is the first Act
> The second, loss,
> Third, Expedition for
> the "Golden Fleece"

[28] Ford, *Heaven Beguiles the Tired*, p. 117.
[29] *Ibid.*, p. 117.

Fourth, no Discovery—
Fifth, no Crew—
Finally, no Golden Fleece—
Jason—sham—too.

870

Yet she still kept asking the same kind of questions
at the end of her life as she did in the early years. Do
those about to die experience some vision? Does con-
templation of the physical aspects of the corpse lead
to a glimpse of eternity? "Is there more than Love
and Death? Tell me its name!" As Thomas Johnson
has suggested: "She herself never really understood
that she had answered her questions by the act of
creating her poems."[30]

Her difficulty was not so much with her subject
nor even with herself in her various Child roles. It
was the audience.

[30] Johnson, *Interpretive Biography*, p. 207.

[83]

CHAPTER IV

The Audience

🌼 *A Letter always feels to me like immortality.*
. . . . there seems a spectral power in thought that
walks alone—

II, *330*

BECAUSE OF EMILY DICKINSON's singular mode of existence, the impersonal nature of much of her poetry, the critical emphasis on her timelessness and universality, and the sentimental legend which has developed over the years, the poet has generally been considered to have been isolated from the tensions and conflicts of her nation, insulated from the drama of Amherst, detached in her poetry from the stresses of normal living, and utterly alone. Sometimes Emily encouraged such notions. In April, 1853, she wrote:

The Newmans [cousins of the poet] seem very pleas-
ant, but they are not like us. What makes a few of

us so different from others? It's a question I often ask
myself.

I, 118

Again, nine years later Emily wrote in a poem

> The Soul selects her own Society—
> Then—shuts the Door—
> To her divine Majority—
> Present no more—

303

But not even Emily Dickinson was capable of such
stringent economy. She also wrote

> Between My Country—and the Others—
> There is a Sea—
> But Flowers—negotiate between us—
> As Ministry.

905

Fortunately the "Flowers" acting as ambassadors
most often accompanied poems and letters or, in the
metaphorical sense, the "Flowers" were the letters
themselves. At any rate Emily Dickinson needed an
audience, whether merely to keep in touch with the
world, or to give comfort in bearing still another
death, or for support in bearing that heaviest of all
burdens—her own genius. Whatever the need might
have been, it is never more clearly revealed than in a
letter she wrote in 1866 to Mrs. Josiah Holland.

[85]

Mrs. Holland had made the mistake of addressing a letter to *both* Lavinia and Emily. The poet's reply is to the point.

A mutual plum is not a plum. I was too respectful to take the pulp and do not like a stone.

Send no union letters. The soul must go by Death alone, so, it must by life, if it is a soul.

If a committee—no matter.

II, 321

Surprising in its tone, this letter reveals the poet who was capable of handing down royal pronouncements, and the person who needed to establish lines of communication with other human beings. The very fact that this is a letter demonstrates what those lines of communication are to be.

Rightly insisting that Emily Dickinson was an inveterate letter writer, David Higgins has asserted that what she undertook was "society-by-mail."[1] Although this is true in the sense that she did conduct intimate friendships by mail with the letters serving as a kind of conversation, an equally important function of the letters was that they provided her an audience, limited, admittedly, in number but still an audience on her own terms. An audience-by-mail.

[1] David Higgins, *Portrait of Emily Dickinson: The Poet and Her Prose* (Brunswick, N.J.: Rutgers University Press, 1967), p. 6.

In fact, the societal function, claimed by Higgins, seems almost secondary when we recall Emily's statements, first in the preceding letter—'that the soul must go by life and death alone'—and then in the opening quotation to this chapter: "A letter . . . is the mind alone without corporeal friend." What she needed was not so much a "pen-pal"—which, in her case, would have been someone to challenge her spark of genius with his own—but rather she needed listeners to the problems she encountered as a human being, spectators to her method of problem-solving through her poetry, and support for the burden of her genius. As an ancient riddler must surely have required an audience to appreciate his art in over-coming an opponent, she needed appreciation as an artist of the riddle.

That she approached letter-writing and life in much the same way—as an artist who chose to present herself deliberately to an audience—is evident first from her method of letter composition, then from her method of audience confrontation. Higgins has shown that a given letter might have been begun years before in her workshop, that "scrap basket" collection of prose and poetic fragments collected through the years and then smoothly integrated into letters.[2] No matter how personal her grief at the

[2] *Ibid.*, pp. 6–7.

death of a friend, she was enough of an artist to incorporate the same poems, sentences or words for other appropriate occasions. The following poem, a parody of a letter, indicates how she regarded the flatness of most correspondence.

> Bee! I'm expecting you!
> Was saying Yesterday
> To Somebody you know
> That you were due—
>
> The Frogs got Home last Week—
> Are settled, and at work—
> Birds, mostly back—
> The Clover warm and thick—
>
> You'll get my Letter by
> The seventeenth; Reply
> Or better, be with me—
> Yours, Fly.
>   *1035*

And when she chose to meet her audience face to face she must have had magnificent stage-presence. The occasion might be a full-scale dramatic performance. Higginson, in a letter to his wife, describes one such performance.

A step like a pattering child's in entry & in glided a little plain woman with two smooth bands of reddish

hair & a face a little like Belle Dove's; not plainer—
with no good feature—in a very plain & exquisitely
clean white pique & a blue net worsted shawl. She
came to me with two day lilies which she put in a
sort of childlike way into my hand & said "These are
my introduction" in a soft frightened breathless child-
like voice—& added under her breath Forgive me if
I am frightened; I never see strangers & hardly know
what I say—

II, 342a

Undoubtedly such a performance drained Higginson's nerve power as he told his wife in another
letter. And if T. W. Higginson found his first meeting with the poet debilitating, Emily found almost
all personal confrontations extremely exhausting
and, therefore, usually avoided them. In lieu of personal contact with people, she could compose a letter
at her leisure; a letter need not make her self-con-
scious; in a letter she did not need to make adjust-
ments to the recipient's tone of voice or gesture. To
use a cliché, audience-by-mail enabled her to "have
her cake and eat it, too."

She seems always to have enjoyed letter-writing
whether or not the recipient answered in kind. But
when in her thirties she began including poetry on a
fairly regular basis in her letter, she must have done
so because she had already discovered how much
letter-writing aided her in obtaining an audience on

her own terms. She may have been encouraged in this view of the value of a letter by one of her favorite writers, Ik Marvel (D. G. Mitchell). In *Reveries of a Bachelor* (1851) he wrote

> Blessed be letters!— . . . they are the only true hearttalkers! . . . . Your truest thought is modified half through its utterance by a look, a sign, a smile, or a sneer . . . . But it is not so of Letters: there you are, with only the soulless pen, and the snow-white virgin paper. Your soul is measuring itself by itself and saying its own saying: . . . nothing is present, but you, and your thought.[3]

Why was audience-by-mail peculiarly advantageous to her? As has been suggested, it gave her the contact with the world that is necessary to an artist; it was not so debilitating as being continually "on" for a live audience. On the personal level it meant reassurances about the last moments of dead friends. Artistically, these reassurances about the friends meant a means of bringing the dead back by offering the point of view of another person which she could incorporate into her poetry.[4] The final and unique asset of an audience-by-mail was that it acted as a support to the lonely burden of her own genius. Although such friends as the Norcross cousins, Mrs.

[3] Higgins, *Portrait of Emily Dickinson*, p. 74.
[4] *Ibid.*, pp. 183–184.

Josiah Holland and later Mabel Loomis Todd
could, through their love and trust, help her bear the
moments of her creative power—"Eternity's Disclo-
sure" in words, "The Colossal substance of Immortality"—, she relied on a series of "Preceptors" for
assurance that her ability was authentic. Foremost
among these was Colonel T. W. Higginson whom
the poet first contacted in 1862 after she read his
"Letters to a Young Contributor" in the *Atlantic
Monthly*. The opening lines from her introductory
letter to Higginson, dated April, 1862, indicate what
his function as an audience is to be.

> *Are you too deeply occupied to say if my Verse
> is alive?*
> *The Mind is so near itself—it cannot see, dis-
> tinctly—and I have none to ask—*
> *Should you think it breathed—and had you the
> leisure to tell me, I should feel quick gratitude—*
>   II, *260*

If Emily Dickinson required an audience for her
art and life, she was willing to make certain conces-
sions to acquire her special type of audience. In analyzing the intellectual capacities of her correspondents and adapting her own style to the individual, in
the great care and deliberate composition of each
letter, she may have salvaged a great deal for art
from a rather meagre and, by twentieth century

[91]

standards, hopeless existence. However, she had to pay a high price for the audience she chose. Because she found it necessary to cater to correspondents like the Norcross cousins, she left to posterity a series of ridiculous, childish facsimiles of herself in prose. Because she chose Helen Hunt Jackson for an audience, she herself was erroneously conjectured to be the author of Mrs. Jackson's *Saxe Holm* stories. Because she chose Higginson for a literary audience, she was discouraged from publication and missed in her own lifetime the possibility of the "rewarding person."

What seems genuinely tragic in Emily Dickinson's search for the right audience was not so much her errors in judgment as that she was so close to the intellectual currents of her time, so close to the "rewarding person," so close to the "New England Olympus," and yet so hopelessly remote from them all. By pointing out that "at a certain level of New England society everyone knew everyone else" (or, we might add, was related), Higgins has put his finger on the heart of the tragedy. Higgins summarizes the relationship in this way:

> Those correspondents [of Emily Dickinson] who were not well known themselves were usually close to the New England Olympus. Maria Whitney who was in love with Samuel Bowles and a relative of his wife, was the sister of three notable

men—one of them the Yale philologist William Dwight Whitney. . . . Emily's aunt Catherine Sweetser had received love letters from Beecher. Franklin B. Sanborn was a friend and biographer of Thoreau. Higginson's first wife was closely related to Ellery and William Ellery Channing. Mrs. Lucius Boltwood was a cousin of Emerson. Mabel Loomis Todd corresponded with Howells and the Thoreau family; her father, Eben J. Loomis (to whom Emily wrote several notes) had been a companion of Thoreau and Whitman. Emily's girlhood friend Emily Fowler was a granddaughter of Noah Webster.[5]

Actually, with the closeness of relationships to the truly great men of letters which Higgins has shown, it seems a phenomenal piece of bad luck that Emily Dickinson missed in her lifetime the recognition which she craved and deserved.

While it is not the purpose of this paper to belabor the inadequacies of T. W. Higginson as literary preceptor, still a contrast between Higginson's aid, or lack of it, to Emily Dickinson and William Dean Howells' aid to Henry James seems significant. In *Turn West, Turn East*, H. S. Canby has summarized the importance of Howells to James. "[Howells] helped James gain confidence in seeking an audience. . . . [Howells] was an expert in what was

[5] *Ibid.*, pp. 13–14.

being written and could be published . . . a friend worth having."⁶ One wonders how James would have fared at the hands of Higginson, especially in the light of Higginson's one essay on "Henry James, Jr." (1879) in which he wrote: "he [James] should employ someone else to write the last few pages. . . . The reader is left discontented."⁷ Similarly, it is difficult not to conjecture that Emily Dickinson would have fared somewhat differently had she turned to W. D. Howells instead of to T. W. Higginson.⁸

However, the closest that she could come to Howells was Mabel Loomis Todd, who corresponded with him, and who proved to be one of Emily's own better choices as a correspondent. Having recorded the recollections of Austin and Lavinia, collected hundreds of Dickinson's letters, and published the poems, Mrs. Todd is still a primary source of Dickinson scholarship. It is to Mabel Loomis Todd's credit that whatever she may have lacked in

---

⁶ H. S. Canby, *Turn West, Turn East* (Boston: Houghton Mifflin Co., 1951), p. 73.

⁷ F. W. Dupee, ed., *The Question of Henry James* (New York: Henry Holt & Co., 1945), p. 5.

⁸ Lars Åhnebrink, *The Beginning of Naturalism in American Fiction* (New York: Russell & Russell, 1961), pp. 94–95. Åhnebrink, in pointing out that Howells had inspired Stephen Crane to write his first book of poetry by reading aloud some of Dickinson's poems, has underscored the irony in Emily's choice of Higginson rather than Howells.

editorial ability or critical judgment, she made up for in her enthusiasm and patience in carrying out a very difficult piece of work.

A brief examination of Dickinson's correspondence with Mrs. Todd illuminates the poet's method when she suspected that she had encountered the rewarding person and provides a possible answer to why we must not guess the riddle of the poem that she sent to Higginson.

> The Riddle that we guess
> We speedily despise—
> Not anything is stale so long
> As Yesterday's Surprise—
>
> II, *353*

Believing that "Human Nature dotes/on what it can't detect" she found in riddle the perfect method not only for a poet who was essentially childlike and whose subject was death, but also the chief technique for the poet who would keep an audience-by-mail. When we realize that the poet's letters of her last years resemble games of guess-what-I-am-thinking with the number of puzzles dependent on the recipient,[9] and then apply this standard to Dickinson's correspondence with Mabel Loomis Todd, we see how Emily used riddles to bind an intellectually curious and appreciative audience to her. Indicative

[9] Whicher, *This Was A Poet*, p. 147.

of the high regard the poet had for Mrs. Todd as an audience and the extreme lengths to which Emily could carry ambiguity is the following:

> Nature forgot—The Circus reminded her—
> Thanks for the Ethiopian Face.
> The Orient is in the West.
> 'You knew, Oh Egypt' said the entangled Antony—
>
> III, 978

Who would ever guess that this is a thank-you note for a yellow jug painted by Mabel Todd and given to Emily Dickinson?[10]

Since letters were a part of her art, her conversation, her autobiography, we should not be surprised that the letters are a key to why a childlike poet whose subject was death should choose to write in riddle. The same mind conceived both the poetry and the prose. To Emily Dickinson, person and poet, the audience was indispensable.

[10] Leyda, *The Years and Hours of Emily Dickinson,* 2:446.

CHAPTER V

The Wider Audience

❧ *I hear robins a great way off, and wagons a great way off, and rivers a great way off, and all appear to be hurrying somewhere undisclosed to me. Remoteness is the founder of sweetness; could we see all we hope, or hear the whole we fear told tranquil, like another tale, there would be madness near. Each of us gives or takes heaven in corporeal person, for each of us has the skill of life.*

II, *388*

INDEED, WHEN EMILY DICKINSON SAID, "A letter always feels to me like immortality . . . ," we may suppose that she meant us, her wider audience, to accept this statement at face value. For it was with this child of the nineteenth century as with so many of her contemporaries and indeed with her successors in this present time that the traditional Chris-

tian concept of a bodily Resurrection was held
suspect by the findings of the physical sciences and
notably by the impact of the works of Charles Darwin. In fact, this keystone of the Christian faith
seems alternately to have beckoned and baffled the
poet through its comfort and absurdity. Expressive
of the bafflement which every rational man must experience in the face of the idea of Deity and of
Resurrection, yet indicative, too, of the longing which
one might feel for its solace is the following poem,
penned late in the poet's life:

> Those—dying then,
> Knew where they went—
> They went to God's Right Hand—
> That Hand is amputated now
> And God cannot be found—
>
> The abdication of Belief
> Makes the Behavior small—
> Better an ignis fatuus
> Than no illume at all—
>
> *1551*

And if God seemed dead or His Resurrection elusive,
a scientific or cosmic concept of immortality was
equally untenable.

When Emily Dickinson found the route of reason and the affirmation of faith alike unsatisfactory,

she could write poetry in which she used the conflict-
ing ideologies as material for her art. She could
employ the strategy of verbal conflict; she could, in
short, write riddles. One of the earliest and finest of
her poems underscores the conflict between a traditional Christian view of the Resurrection and a kind
of astronomical concept of eternity. Significantly, her
preference for either viewpoint remains an enigma;
in fact, according to Charles Anderson's reading of
"Alabaster Chambers" she may actually have preferred the humanist's view of life as "signalized by
the use of the exclamation point" in the 1859 stanza.[1]

> Safe in their Alabaster Chambers—
> Untouched by Morning
> And untouched by Noon—
> Sleep the meek members of the Resurrection—
> Rafter of satin,
> And Roof of stone.
>
> Light laughs the breeze
> In her Castle above them—
> Babbles the Bee in a stolid Ear,
> Pipe the Sweet Birds in ignorant cadence—
> Ah, what sagacity perished here!
>
> *216, 1859*

[1] Charles R. Anderson, *Emily Dickinson's Poetry:
Stairway of Surprise* (New York: Holt, Rinehart & Winston, 1960), pp. 270–271.

> Grand go the Years—in the Crescent—above
>   them—
> Worlds scoop their Arcs—
> And Firmaments—row—
> Diadems—drop—and Doges—surrender—
> Soundless as dots—on a Disc of Snow—
>
> *216*, 1861

Though she could never reconcile the Resurrection
and cosmic extinction—or "Alabaster Chambers"
with the "Disc of Snow"—still she was vitally interested in the issue of immortality, whatever its nature
might be. So absorbed, in fact, was she with this
subject that she recorded a conversation about it in a
letter written to Mrs. J. G. Holland, dated July,
1880. Emily Dickinson wrote:

> *Austin and I were talking the other Night about the
> Extension of Consciousness, after Death and Mother
> told Vinnie, afterward, she thought it was "very im-
> proper."*
>
> III, *650*

Improper as this subject may have seemed to her
parents' generation, or to "those dying then" who
still "knew where they went," it was a crucial subject
to one who desired more and more with the passing
of time to perpetuate something of the essential self

against mutation, who coveted, as it were, a type of immortality. And if immortality was not to be found in a traditional resurrection or in a vast, cold cosmic union, where was it then to be found? The development of Emily Dickinson's concern for and concept of immortality is, if not in itself unique, certainly a clarification of such problems surrounding this poet as her use of riddle, her decision not to publish and, especially, her choice of audience.

When one attempts to analyze what Emily Dickinson came to realize as "immortality," one again meets a riddle. Essentially the enigma that confounded Emily Dickinson, in perceiving the implications of immortality, was whether it was in some sense personal or in lyrics to be preserved for posterity. Indicative of her preoccupation with and conflict over these seeming polar positions on the subject are excerpts from the letters and poems. For instance, an often quoted passage from one of her letters goes ". . . we are mentally permanent. 'It is finished' can never be said of us." (ii, 555) and would seem to be a triumphant assertion in favor of a kind of personal immortality. Again, and significantly, the last letter that she wrote shortly before her death admits a dual interpretation relevant to this problem. To the Norcross sisters, Emily wrote simply "Called back." Certainly, the poet had been called back or had escaped once again the final crisis of her physical illness; yet, given the poet's partiality toward word plays and double meanings, this terse message may quite properly refer also to Hugh Conway's *Called Back*, a popular book of that period which Emily had read and which concerned her preoccupation—the extension of consciousness beyond death. In still another letter written toward the end of her life, she suggested another type of immortality and the impossibility of ever achieving it. The well-known and wryly humorous "Biography first convinces us of the fleeing of the Biographied—"(III, 972) is typical of her use of double meanings and of her preoccupation with the problem of immortality. What Dickinson seems to have meant by this characteristically cryptic statement is that not only does the body flee the biographer but, more important, the essence or the spirit of the person tends to elude the biographer as well. Fascinated by the possibility of some kind of permanence beyond death but vacillating between positions of mental permanence and a continuity of consciousness which she, in a famous poem, termed "Costumeless," she firmly decided against the kind of immortality offered by "biographers," or, in other words, against the songs of posterity. Essentially uncertain of individual immortality, unwilling to trust the kind of immortality offered by fame or the songs of posterity, she turned instinctively to the only kind of immortality which was tenable to her.

In the light of Emily Dickinson's search for and understanding of immortality it is not only appropriate that her last letter should exhibit the poet's preoccupation, but it is especially significant that she chose a letter as the final form of her preoccupation. It is perhaps not too extravagant to say that the letter represented for Emily Dickinson the one kind of immortality that she could most reasonably realize. Not satisfied herself with the death riddles which she set for others, nor willing to accept the dictum she established in an 1864 poem, "Had I the curiosity/ 'Twere not appeased of men/ Till Resurrection, I must guess" (876), she chose, quite simply, neither to guess nor even to wait. Rather she seems instinctively and audaciously to have established her own poetic manifesto, as well as to have foreshadowed the immortality she sought, in these famous early lines:

> This is my letter to the World
> That never wrote to Me—
> The simple News that Nature told—
> With tender Majesty
>
> Her Message is committed
> To Hands I cannot see—
> For love of Her—Sweet—countrymen—
> Judge tenderly—of Me
>
> 441

Later then she attempted to formulate the importance of letters to her when she wrote "A letter always feels to me like immortality . . ." and, in so doing, shed light for us on why we should indeed think of her poetry as letters to the world, or brave attempts to achieve for herself immortality on her own terms. Again, her final letter may simply reaffirm her preoccupation with the subject, or it may more significantly serve to remind us that "Called back" emphatically and explicitly states where a poet of the calibre of Emily Dickinson might expect to achieve immortality: *in this world.* Incapable of accepting an extension of consciousness beyond death which is in the person, or at least individual, unwilling to accept immortality wholly in the songs of posterity, she chose what for her was the only alternative: lyrics written through letters to posterity, or what one might term, the immortality of the Letter.

Surprisingly the early preference for the earth as indicated by the 1859 version of the famous "Alabaster Chambers" and the kind of immortality best achieved through letters sent to the world do not give way at the end of the poet's life to a reaffirmation of a traditional faith. The following poem, sent in a letter to the Norcross sisters in 1884, near the end of Dickinson's life, renders again the aching and now imminent problem of the elusive resurrection.

The going from a world we know
To one a wonder still
Is like the child's adversity
Whose vista is a hill,
Behind the hill is sorcery
And everything unknown,
But will the secret compensate
For climbing it alone?

1603

This poem, written late in the poet's life, together with the 1859 version of "Alabaster Chambers" written early in her career and indicating an early concern with this life and this world, seems to point once again to why Emily Dickinson might even come to prefer the kind of immortality implicit in letters written to the world rather than the Christian concept of immortality which she suggests is like a cold, white prison offered to the "meek members of the Resurrection." The key to Dickinson's problem as a person who was also a poet is to be found in the last word of the preceding poem—in the word "alone." If the immortality offered by science does away with "aloneness," it also annihilates the individual, merging him into some kind of vast, nebulous cosmic union as the poet has suggested in the final stanza of "Alabaster Chambers"; on the other hand, the immortality of the Christian Resurrection—at least as

Emily understood it—was, if achievable, essentially a lonely, perhaps comfortless, experience. The agonizing dilemma for Emily Dickinson was, of course, that she desired above all else, both in her human life and in her grand gamble with a hereafter to perpetuate something of the essential self and to maintain an audience as well.

Although the poem which begins "This is my letter to the World" has been much quoted and has, in fact, been evaluated as important or even pivotal to Dickinson's art, emphasis has not been placed where it would surely seem to belong; special attention has not, in short, been accorded to the role of the audience in the poet's characteristic concerns and in her art. Yet in this poem, perhaps, more clearly than in any other poem, Emily Dickinson signifies her audience, names it as "the World" and even indicates the single most important characteristic of that wider audience which accounts for much that is enigmatic in the poet's own work. In a line of great moment, she writes quite simply, even flatly, that it is to be of audiences the most frustrating, the most difficult and paradoxically the most demanding: it is to be the audience "who never wrote to me."

The choice of an audience wider than her circle of friends, wider than her town, wider even than her own time; in fact, the choice of the widest possible audience, the choice of posterity seems now to the twentieth century reader of Emily Dickinson both an inevitable and an inspired choice. Certainly, it must seem inevitable when one recalls the poet's isolation from the main artistic currents of her time or when one recalls Colonel Higginson's incessant advice not to publish or, perhaps most crucial, when one recalls the alterations which occurred in the few poems published during the poet's life. Posterity as audience becomes credible, too, as one analyzes Emily Dickinson's concern as person and poet with the riddle of death. If as Emily asserted in one poem "This world is not Conclusion," but " 'Heaven'—is what I cannot Reach!", if Emily Dickinson was in George Whicher's inspired image a kind of "metaphysical ballerina" precariously balanced between the polar positions of resurrection and annihilation, her only fulcrum between these opposed forces, her only tenable position between these poles must involve a radical redefinition in artistic terms of immortality. At first instinctively, then more surely, Emily Dickinson discovered that immortality was paradoxically grounded for her in the fabric of this world. "A letter always feels to me like immortality" she wrote and consequently her poetry indeed became her "letter to the World," her "Bulletins all Day/ From Immortality." If she deplored the perishing of sagacity, denied

[107]

the annihilation of consciousness, and doubted a cosmic concept of eternity, she could respond to the artist's strategy for comprehending immortality. Just as the spider, her symbol for the artist in the following poem, is the source of his own web that becomes his symbol, so the artist is the source of the outward designs he uses to designate inner and eternal values.

> A Spider sewed at Night
> Without a Light
> Upon an Arc of White.
>
> If Ruff it was of Dame
> Or Shroud of Gnome
> Himself himself inform.
>
> Of Immortality
> His Strategy
> Was Physiognomy.
>   *1138*

Characteristically, the poem is cast in the form of a riddle: Has the spider woven a "Ruff for a Dame" or a "Shroud for a Gnome," or, more to the point, can immortality be spun from the stuff of the self?

If a traditional resurrection proved elusive, the artist's concept of immortality, self-realized, was wrought with risk. And the chief element of risk inherent in relying on the immortality of letters written to the world was not so much in the letters, that is in the artistry of the poems themselves, but in the hazard of determining precisely to whom she was writing. It may be very well to write letters to the world, it may even be inspired and audacious to leave lyrics to posterity, but, more to the point, what will be the nature of an audience designated by an all-inclusive abstraction: "the World"? To what will such an audience listen? How, indeed, can it be made to listen? And most poignant—what should be the voice of the speaker who speaks to the audience "who never spoke to me"?

Faced with these puzzles, Emily Dickinson, upon occasion, seemed to feel a reservation about her unorthodox and precarious strategy. In an enigmatic letter to her Norcross cousins, written in September, 1880, Emily tried to express something of the tenuous and terrible power implicit for her in letters.

What is it that instructs a hand lightly created, to impel shapes to eyes at a distance, which for them have the whole area of life or of death? Yet not a pencil in the street but has this awful power, though nobody arrests it. An earnest letter is or should be life-warrant or death-warrant, for what is each instant but a gun, harmless because "unloaded," but that touched "goes off"?

III, *656*

[109]

And again she expressed her reservations more succinctly in a letter written in August 1885 to T. W. Higginson.

> *What a Hazard a Letter is! . . . I almost fear to lift my Hand to so much as a Superscription.*
>
> III, 1007

Indeed the kind of letters Emily Dickinson had in mind were hazardous just because so much depended on the recipient. Emily's strategy for immortality quite literally depended on the selection of the right audience. And in writing for that widest of all audiences, in writing for posterity, in dispatching letters to the world, her instinct proved sound, her judgment was inspired and her poetry proved more enduring than the spider's filament, which for her symbolized the immortality to which she aspired.

Because Emily Dickinson was so intoxicated with the sense of being alive, she chose to solve the riddle of death through the art of her poetry, or this having proved a hopeless quest, she, at least, hoped to assure herself a voice in the future, a place beyond provincial nineteenth-century New England. If, as Emily Dickinson seemed to believe, "an earnest letter is or should be a Life warrant or a Death warrant," then she would infinitely have preferred that her letter to the world should be a life warrant—should, in fact, insure that that breathless, insistent,

small New England voice never be extinguished.
Indicative of her high regard for the individual
human consciousness as well as of the direction to
which her life and art had turned is the following
poem, appearing toward the close of her life in a
letter dated June, 1877.

> Such are the inlets of the mind—
> His outlets—would you see
> Ascend with me the eminence
> Of immortality—
>
> *1421*

Especially significant in this poem is the invocation
of that wider audience—signified simply as "you"—
to join the poet in her quest, an invocation which is
an authentic invitation for community or fellowship
in the search for permanence and place beyond the
temporal and physical. And in another poem which
has often been considered whimsical or even self-dep-
recating, the poet may also express exactly the degree of intensity of her preoccupation with immortality.

> If nothing larger than a World's
> Departure from a Hinge
> Or Sun's extinction, be observed
> 'Twas not so large that I
> Could lift my Forehead from my work
> For Curiosity.
>
> *985*

[111]

Though couched in terms of exaggeration, there is a deep vein of truth implicit in this poem; eclipses and annihilation are dwarfed before the poet's intense preoccupation, necessary for her ascent to that other paradise: the paradise of art.

Implicit in what Dickinson termed simply in the preceding poem "my work," or, in other words, what she seemed to realize about the choice of posterity as audience, as well as the choices of death as subject and immortality as objective, was first of all the enormity of the artistic problem: How to insure a reading? In essence, if she were to regard her lyrics as letters written to posterity, she must find a method of writing which would, at once, insure a reading for these letters as well as assure, or at least structurally support, whatever meanings she chose to communicate. Again, the poet's use of riddle served as the only method which could satisfy the artistic problem of insuring a reading which would assure the meaning. Because the riddle tends to attract an intellectually avid audience and because, in the hands of an artist, it truly is an inspired strategy to exploit both structurally and semantically the essential ambiguity of the subject of Death, it is the one method which satisfies both facets of the artistic problem.

Intimately connected with the artistic problem of insuring a reading for her lyrics, was the most basic problem of all which the poet faced. How, in fact, could Emily Dickinson insure the bare survival of her poems? In a perceptive essay on this poet, Archibald MacLeish calls our attention to the peculiarly paradoxical way in which Emily chose to insure the bare existence of her poetry. MacLeish reminds us that Emily Dickinson chose to commit

> that live voice of hers to a private box full of snippets of paper—old bills, invitations to commencements, clippings from newspapers—tied together with little loops of thread. . . . Emily locked away in a chest a voice which speaks to every living creature of the things which every living creature knows . . . .[2]

If insuring survival of her work by assigning it to "a private box full of snippets" seems unusually perverse even for the poet who declared that "Publication—is the Auction/ Of the Mind of Man—" the method would also prove to have been inspired. In order to understand why she chose such a peculiar method of survival for her art, one should review her attitude toward success. Much has been written, for example, about Emily's attitude toward success, about her vacillation between seeking literary renown and abrogating it. If publishing seemed some-

[2] Archibald MacLeish, "The Private World: Poems of Emily Dickinson," From *Poetry and Experience* (Boston: Houghton Mifflin Co., 1961).

times as "foreign as Firmament to Fin," she also understood, rather ruefully perhaps, that "Success" was an "aim forever touched with dew." And again she seemed almost to have accepted a stoic position when she wrote that "If fame belonged to me, I could not escape her." Deprived of recognition during her own lifetime, compensating for this deprivation by writing for posterity, Emily Dickinson seems finally to have come to the belief that the ability of her art, her letters to the world, simply to survive was the only true measure of their greatness. Apparently she came to feel, too, that her art could not survive through any of the conventional channels of publication, for these involved artistic compromise; still her work might survive—and with artistic integrity—by simply being preserved, nearly two thousand poems of it, in that private box.

That survival by consignment to a box, if extremely idiosyncratic, will ultimately secure for the poet the kind of universal reading she desired must depend, finally, on what is consigned to that box. In essence, if Emily Dickinson had to insure survival for her work as well as to consider the best method to secure a reading, she had also to determine what her audience would listen to. In her choice of chaotic, cryptic manuscripts for preservation, she was trying not so much to repudiate an earthly audience as to attract the universal audience. In retrospect this seems to have been a truly inspired solution to the problem of the "message" of her work.

Although the chronological riddle, or the problem of dating the poems, has to a large extent been solved by the work of Thomas H. Johnson, twentieth-century readers of Emily Dickinson still find her letters to the world riddled with enigma. There is, for instance, the riddle of selecting from all the variants of a given poem the poet's so-called final reading. Since she did not choose to publish, we do not know when a fair copy is "intermediary" or "final"; in short, we have no terminus for any given poem since she never committed herself to the finality of publication. Likewise the enigma of her idiosyncratic handwriting has never been completely solved. Numerous theories have been devised to account for the capitals, dashes and peculiarities of syntax; for instance, John Crowe Ransom has declared that Dickinson's capital letters were her way of conferring dignity and are, in fact, a "mythopoetic device." And Charles R. Anderson theorizes that the poet's punctuation is "a new system of musical notation for reading," while Edith Perry Stamm demonstrates convincingly that Emily Dickinson's mechanics are designed to inform the reader of how to declaim a given poem. Nonetheless, R. W. Franklin casts some doubt on the total acceptance of any one or all of these theories. Franklin points out that these same devices are peculiar not only to Dickinson's poems but also to the poet's more domestic concerns; namely, household notes, shopping lists and recipes. They would seem, according to Franklin's view, to be merely a habit of her handwriting.[3]

What Emily Dickinson intended concerning her poems after her death, we can only infer from her attitude toward immortality, from specific letters and poems which strongly suggest that she thought intently about a wider audience and especially from the chaotic and cryptic messages consigned to that private box which became her letter to the world. In firmly and consistently failing to choose from among her variants, in not indicating the significance of the mechanics of her handwriting and in neglecting even to date her poems, Emily Dickinson was not being merely eccentric but was attempting to insure that posterity—"Those fair-fictitious People"—would listen, would indeed participate with the poet in determining to what they would listen by selecting, arranging and interpreting her letter to the world. Because it necessitates participation by the audience, Emily Dickinson would probably have applauded the spirit of the kind of participation implicit in R. W. Franklin's call for a "reader's edition" of her

[3] R. W. Franklin, *The Editing of Emily Dickinson: A Reconsideration* (Madison: University of Wisconsin Press, 1967), pp. 120–128.

poems, though she may indeed have been apprehensive of the end product. Franklin concludes that what is needed for a reader's edition of the poems is

the development and demonstration of a new editorial procedure for material unprepared by the author for publication. . . . Poems are neither self-generating nor self-maturing, and those which lack completion by Emily Dickinson will have to be finished by an editor. That editor . . . will have to struggle with editorial and critical principles even to the limits of ontology and epistemology. He will be editor, critic, and philosopher in one.[4]

Still, though Emily Dickinson's letter to the world seems curiously open-ended because of her subject, choice of audience and method of obtaining a reading, her poetry does, as it now stands, communicate meaning, or rather it communicates multiple meanings. If her poetry does not "codify nature's signals" or attempt to answer the question "What does this signify?" in the face of every experience, it does, as Archibald MacLeish has written, deal with "the human experience and its object" is humanity.[5] What she seems to say about the human experience by her strategy of riddle, allusive imagery and am-

[4] *Ibid.*, pp. 142–143.
[5] MacLeish, "The Private World."

[117]

biguous symbol, and by failing to provide a precise context necessary for a definitive reading, is that it is at best complex and ambiguous and that the reader must bring to a reading of her poems inferences based on his own experience, that the audience must provide the context, must, in fact, develop "the undeveloped freight/ of a/ delivered syllable."[6] Indeed, this verbal equivalent of expressionism in painting is likewise compatible with another thoroughly "modern" tenet of her art: the impotence of language to frame human experience. The following poem may, as Donald Thackrey indicates, signify that "the truly significant things in human experience dwelled in the realm of silence and secrecy," and that "human communication was unavailing before the greatness of the universe and the complexity of man's experience within it."[7]

> I found the words to every thought
> I ever had—but One—
> And that—defies me—
> As a Hand did try to chalk the Sun

[6] In *The Art of Emily Dickinson's Early Poetry*, David Porter compares the poet's reliance on an audience for context to the equivalent of *sfumato*, an expressionistic painting technique which requires the viewer to supply out of his own imagination the context for a painting, p. 99.

[7] Donald E. Thackrey, "The Communication of the Word," from *Emily Dickinson's Approach to Poetry* (Lincoln: University of Nebraska Studies, 1954).

To Races—nurtured in the Dark—
How would your own—begin?
Can Blaze be shown in Cochineal—
Or Noon—in Mazarin?

581

If we do not find a philosophy of life, a rationale for existence, cogent or coherent answers to the great questions posed by the humanities in Emily Dickinson's poems, we can discover, if we, her wider audience, listen, something else which serves to enrich the content of human experience. What we can hear is the "authentic voice" which penetrates to the quick of a particular emotion, whose poetry does not so much mirror experience but becomes experience and in "exist(ing) independent of the confining facts of exterior experience . . . becomes thereby increasingly universal."[8] In essence, that which universalizes the poetry of Emily Dickinson and ultimately has assured her the wider audience she craved is the voice, which, expressing multiple meanings by methods which exploit ambiguity, can still speak directly across time and space to the particular person about the common lot of us all.

If, as Archibald MacLeish has described it in his definition of poetry as "universal words, generalizations, abstractions made particular in a particular

[8] Porter, *The Art of Emily Dickinson's Early Poetry*, p. 175.

voice,"[9] then Emily Dickinson was correct in her assertion that "It is finished can never be said of us." By method, by meaning and by voice, Emily Dickinson has done all that one could well do to insure the permanence of her art and thus to ascend to that other paradise, the artist's conception of immortality. And because she chose to write of the inscrutability of God, the inviolability of the self and the anguish before the riddle of death—common concerns of humanity—in the spontaneous "live locutions of dramatic speech" and in a tone which abrogates self-pity, the voice is as fresh, as alive today, as when she first consigned to a private box her cryptic letters to the world. Though the voice which speaks to us across time and space is, in fact, many voices, varying even in the same poem from outrage to acquiescence

> Burglar! Banker—Father!
> I am poor once more!
>
> *49*

it is particularly Emily Dickinson's own spontaneous, often ironic, but always authentic voice, just as we hear it in this death riddle.

> Dust is the only Secret—
> Death, the only One
> You cannot find out all about
> In his "native town."

[9] MacLeish, "The Private World."

Nobody knew "his Father"—
Never was a Boy—
Had'nt any playmates,
Or "Early history"—

Industrious! Laconic!
Punctual! Sedate!
Bold as a Brigand!
Stiller than a Fleet!

Builds, like a Bird, too!
Christ robs the Nest—
Robin after Robin
Smuggled to Rest!

153

It is a voice which early discovered that irony, incongruity, detachment and indirection—the tools of the universal comic—was the way to possess the subject of Death, which so often eluded comprehension at deeper levels.

In analyzing Emily Dickinson's strategy for immortality, achieved by sending enigmatic letters to the world—letters which record human experience in an authentic voice—one realizes that a clarification of such human experiences will prove relevant to a study of Dickinson's poetry. In fact, various critics have in the past termed her mystical poet, Transcendentalist, or romantic; and in more recent times she

[121]

has been called existentialist or even modern religious poet—all on the basis of how they read the
human experiences which Emily records. Whether
or not these critical judgments *all* seem sound is not
nearly so important as the fact that such affinities to
so many schools of thought serve emphatically to
underscore the universal appeal of Emily Dickinson's poetry. And it is in the spirit of universalizing
Emily Dickinson's poetry that I offer another facet
by which one may view the human experiences
which the poet recorded for posterity. Although this
study is concerned with the application of riddle, in
itself a traditional apparatus, to the poetry of Emily
Dickinson, there is still a facet of Dickinson's poetry
which is universal in subject as well as modern in
thrust or direction and which makes her art both
appealing and relevant to the present time.

Indeed, she is startlingly modern in her application of techniques to poetry which presently have
become associated with the kinds of modern media
with which Marshall McLuhan concerns himself. In
particular, the impact of the visual images of some of
Dickinson's finest poems is related to the impact of
visual images in certain of our modern cinematic
experiments. Her finest achievement in nature poetry, the eight-line hummingbird poem, reads as a
kind of *tour de force* of these experimental techniques. Here is the poem.

A Route of Evanescence
With a revolving Wheel—
A Resonance of Emerald—
A Rush of Cochineal—
And every Blossom on the Bush
Adjusts it's tumbled Head—
The mail from Tunis, probably,
An easy Morning's Ride—

1463

It has been noted that the total effect of the visual images in this poem is actually related to the photographic process in general. Actually Dickinson's inspired use of visual images represents an inversion of the photographic process: instead of the simultaneous exposure of a moving object, she details the simultaneous vanishing of the object at every point.[10] Then, too, her inspired choice of "revolving Wheel" to describe the hummingbird's wings in motion effects in language a technique which is familiar to directors of experimental films. One notes that "revolving Wheel" presents a kind of optical illusion of the bird's wings, not the actuality. Even more in keeping with the modern cinema, which seems to be moving further and further away from what McLuhan designated as "hot," or "linear" or "high definition," is Emily Dickinson's structuring of this poem

[10] Grover Smith, "Dickinson's 'A Route of Evanescence,'" *The Explicator* 7 (May, 1949): Item 54.

[123]

by visual image instead of by logic. Just as some of
the cinematic experiments give difficulty to an audience accustomed to the cause and effect logic of the
old linear movie, so the terminal lines of Dickinson's
hummingbird poem give her audience difficulty precisely because they lack a logical, coherent, "linear"
relationship with the rest of the poem. And because
the precise nature of what Dickinson had in mind by
"The mail from Tunis, probably,/ An easy Morning's Ride—" remains a riddle, it evokes by its ambiguity a response in her audience. Like McLuhan's
description of "cool" media, it gives a meager
amount of information and relies on the audience
to complete the meaning within the context of
the whole poem. The audience is expected to see
the image of the speeding railway train beyond the
image of the hummingbird, as one critic has said, or,
if one will, to see in the bird's flight from "Tunis" a
breaking of all temporal and spatial barriers. Finally, before turning from this exceptional poem, one
notes that Emily Dickinson's use of language which
evokes simultaneously sound, color and motion is a
kind of precursor of the modern, popular admonition
to mix the media.

Perhaps more significant than experimental techniques involving visual images is another technique
shared by the nineteenth century's artist of indirection and surprise and the twentieth century's experi-

mental art forms such as the cinema and, to a lesser degree, television. It has been noted with perception that the film is strongest when it makes use of what is peculiarly its own—the ability to record time and space, slice them up into fragments and glue them together in new relationships. Emily Dickinson, too, understood this technique and employed it brilliantly in the monumental "Because I could not stop for Death." Particularly arresting in this poem is the kind of new relationship which the poet achieved by her juxtaposition of time and eternity to detail the experience of what it might be like to pass out of human time. "We passed the setting Sun—," she wrote, "Or rather—He passed Us—" which must surely be the experience if one could actually escape out of time. Akin to the technique of radical juxtapositions of time and space shared by Emily Dickinson's poetry and modern experimental media is that of telescoping time. In 1959, Loring Mandell's *Project Immortality* was presented as a television drama in which the audience was given an intimate portrait of the growth of a genius through a series of brief scenes. Even more startling because it is effected simply in a few words is Dickinson's marvelous telescoping of time in the "Because I could not stop for Death" poem. She wrote quite simply "Since then— 'tis Centuries—and yet feels shorter than the Day." In less than a dozen words she managed to telescope the centuries to less than the length of one day, thus effecting the transition from time to eternity.

Most significant to the present study is not so much the similarities of techniques involving visual images and time-space relationships, but the similarities of the purposes for which these experimental techniques are used in both Emily Dickinson's poems and modern experimental media. For instance, both Dickinson in "Because I could not stop for Death" and directors of such modern cinematic experiments as Joyce's *Finnegan's Wake* or the much discussed *2001: Space Odyssey* seem through these radical techniques to be trying to offer meaningful answers to the age-old question: Can an obsession with death, pushed to an extreme, result in some absolute awareness of life?

Emily Dickinson, too, was vitally concerned with the riddle of death precisely because she wanted so intensely to live in whatever sense of the word that should prove possible to her. In a forthright and sibylline voice, her words span now nearly a century:

So I conclude that space and time are things of the body and have little or nothing to do with ourselves. My Country is Truth . . . it is a free Democracy.[11]

[11] Richard B. Sewall, *The Lyman Letters: New Light on Emily Dickinson and Her Family* (Amherst: University of Massachusetts Press, 1963), p. 71.

Emily Dickinson's quest for truth, specifically the truth about death, and the absolute awareness of life to which she aspired show affinities not only with modern concerns but also with the Greek norm to see things steadily and see them whole. Still, "wholes are not to be found here below" she once wrote, and in her ambivalence of attitude, her indecisiveness, her exploitation of ambiguity, she stands with modern writers. Illustrative again of the universal quest for truth and the modern uncertainty about that quest is the following little poem written to her nephew:

> Lad of Athens, faithful be
> To Thyself,
> And Mystery—
> All the rest is Perjury—
> *1768*

If in gazing steadily at the face of death all her artistic life, she discovered the artist's conception of immortality, as well as the nature and importance of the wider audience, she also came to something of an absolute awareness of life, which, if it can be encompassed by words, would seem to reside for posterity in such poems as "I Felt a Funeral in my Brain." Often described as an intimate detailing of the experience of psychic breakdown, it may better serve to demonstrate an awareness of the tenacity with which the human consciousness endeavors to prevail before the finality of death.

I felt a Funeral, in my Brain,
And Mourners to and fro
Kept treading—treading—till it seemed
That Sense was breaking through—

And when they all were seated,
A Service, like a Drum—
Kept beating—beating—till I thought
My Mind was going numb—

And then I heard them lift a Box
And creak across my Soul
With those same Boots of Lead, again,
Then Space—began to toll,

As all the Heavens were a Bell,
And Being, but an Ear,
And I, and Silence, some strange Race
Wrecked, solitary, here—

And then a Plank in Reason, broke,
And I dropped down, and down—
And hit a World, at every plunge,
And Finished knowing—then—

280

Or, paradoxically, the poet indicates that, in order to live, one can simply evade the subject if death defies comprehension.

> While simple-hearted neighbors
> Chat of the "Early dead"—
> We—prone to periphrasis,
> Remark that Birds have fled!
>
> *45*

But in the later years of her life, just as at the inception of her career as poet, Emily Dickinson came to realize that "the riddle of those who resting rise," the dilemma of the human condition, the enunciation of the tragic vision of life can best be handled by cutting wit or irony; in short, by a form of humorous detachment. If the sense of life was so tenacious and the meaning of death could not be fully realized —or for that matter always evaded or even expressed here in this world by indirection and surprise—at least the real incongruities inherent in any awareness of life, Greek or modern, could be expressed by mirth or jest. Just as Emily Dickinson could use humor to possess something she could not feel or understand at a deeper level, such as conventional religion, Resurrection or death, so in completing the cycle of her early years, she came to an awareness of life which was essentially that of the comic vision. She wrote "the truth I do not dare to know I muffle with a jest." Thus she came ultimately to realize that if death could not be "surprised" or plumbed, life could still be tolerated, even relished, by a faithful rendering of the incongruities present in the human condition.

"Each of us gives or takes heaven in corporeal person, for each of us has the skill of life," she wrote. So prodigious was Emily Dickinson's skill of life, her poems, that she grasped *both* alternatives. In "corporeal person" she "took heaven" through her special vision of the artist's concept of immortality. With immortality as the stake, she gambled with posterity and wrote letters to the world. In "corporeal person" she "gave heaven" to posterity through the enduring artistry of her poems—poems which in their enunciation of the quest for the meaning of death offer fresh awareness of the absolute value of life. For Emily Dickinson, the perception of posterity as The Wider Audience was the key to this astonishing double accomplishment.

CHAPTER VI

Conclusion

BECAUSE EMILY DICKINSON, the person and the poet, has seemed to many people as "foreign as firmament to fin," and because riddle, though apparently outside the mainstream of modern literature, has been current through the years in primitive communities, modern folk tradition, and in highly sophisticated literature, a re-evaluation of her life, letters and lyrics in terms of riddle has seemed valid and significant. Using the poet's letter to T. W. Higginson in which she discussed the riddle, both in prose and in poetry, as a factual basis for this study, it has been possible to demonstrate the following points:

(1) that Emily Dickinson used riddles consciously as a language form to express herself ambiguously on such subjects as home, family relationships, nature, nineteenth-century progress, God and death;

(2) that the poet's riddles follow Paull F. Baum's criteria for types of ambiguity which may be found in riddle (intellectual exercise, test of wits and particularly ambiguous answers);

(3) that most of her riddles are properly called "literary riddles" because the answers are relatively unimportant while the contrasting ambiguous elements are extremely important.

It has also been possible to suggest several reasons why Dickinson chose the ambiguity of riddles. The letter to Emily Fowler Ford cited in the introduction (which is itself a riddle) indicates an early love of the form. Although it is now practically impossible to determine which, if indeed any, early books first acquainted the poet with riddles, one can reasonably hypothesize that early primers, the Bible and methods of teaching its content, or possibly even law books may have been that early influence. Certainly, valentines which young people sent each other offered Emily Dickinson occasions to practice riddle making. Then, too, the "life-clock" riddle and its influence on her letters and poetry seem ample evidence that she was aware of riddles and consciously used them. And if one were to read Sir Thomas Browne or Shakespeare, two of her favorite authors, one could perhaps find literary influences for her use of riddle.[1] Although it is not possible to point with any degree of certainty to any one thing within the New England tradition which may have influenced her in the use of riddle, it is possible by examining the poet's life to suggest the major reasons for the use of riddle. Childlike in her ambivalent attitude toward home, family, nature, nineteenth-century progress and God, she chose the form which would allow her to have her say without reprisal. Then, too, the intrinsic ambiguity of her major poetic subject, death, necessitated the use of riddle. Finally, she used riddle to hold—by mail—the special audience which she required as an artist.

In his provocative book, *The Long Shadow*, Clark Griffith summarized Dickinson's transitional position in American literature in this way:

> Emily Dickinson is one of those writers who cause us to see with renewed understanding, the literature that comes both before and after them. She remains one of ours, because her attitudes break with "theirs" and continue to shape—in fact continue to be our own.[2]

Recent work has tended to make her almost exclusively one of "ours," to the point of the recent existen-

---

[1] In *The Letters*, vol. 2, Emily mentions in September 1870 to Higginson that she took *Macbeth* and turned to Birnam Wood, coming twice to Dunsinane (352).

[2] Griffith, *The Long Shadow*, pp. 271.

tial interpretation of her work (*Heaven Beguiles the Tired*). While this may contain an element of truth in illustrating that the work of a great artist can bear almost any construct that the age chooses to impose, Emily Dickinson is in the finest sense of the word one of "theirs," too. Her roots are in the ancient past. This is especially true in her use of the riddle. Hoping to pierce the philosophical, physiological and psychological riddle of death by testing the observable data in her poetry, she makes use of the oldest type of riddle—the ordeal or test. These riddles became a kind of personal ordeal, too. Just as the victim of the so-called neck-riddle hoped to save his life by his answers, so Dickinson hoped to save, not her life, but what amounted to much the same thing, her sanity. But, most of all, the riddles were her artistic ordeal. Through an inspired use of the riddle, Emily Dickinson managed to rejuvenate the language, embody the ambiguity of her subject in a concrete form and maintain the type of audience she required.

However, what began as a complex version of the ancient ordeal became something else. It became a quest, a search for the essential meaning of existence. Sometimes the persistence of the riddle was enough to spur her on; sometimes the puzzlement of the riddle reduced her to the uncertainty of a child and sometimes she realized that it was an expedition into catastrophe. She would not find the golden fleece in this life. Something of the quester's sense of hopelessness of completing the quest is evident in this poem:

> I took my Power in my Hand—
> And went against the World—
> 'Twas not so much as David—had—
> But I—was twice as bold—
>
> I aimed my Pebble—but Myself
> Was all the one that fell—
> Was it Goliah—was too large—
> Or was myself—too small?
>
> *540*

While the riddle escaped solution and the search for meaning proved a hopeless quest, her instinct was sound. Where if not in her riddle poetry was the answer to be found, the meaning to be reached? Thomas Johnson has proved one answer, and, in his failure to explain his provocative statement, has thrown it open to an interpretation relevant to Emily Dickinson's use of the riddle. The statement was this: "She herself never really understood that she had answered her question ["Is there more than Love and Death?"] by the act of creating her poetry."[3] If the meaning of existence is not *in* the poetry but is the *act* of creating it, what is the nature—the mean-

---

[3] Johnson, *Interpretive Biography*, p. 207.

[135]

ing—of that act? In at least one poem, "Further in Summer than the Birds," a riddle poem, the meaning of the poem and the act of creating it are one. Both are ritualistic. If, as Marshall Van Deusen asserts, the poem is an autumnal nature-sacrifice associated with the "pensive custom" of the Christian Mass,[4] and the tone of the whole poem, according to David Porter, is "incantatory,"[5] it is also a riddle poem, for the subject is ambiguous. And one should not be surprised to find the riddle still the *modus* of a poet who can neither understand nature's rituals nor experience the Christian counterparts. Perhaps because she cannot experience the traditional rituals nor understand those of nature, she, like James Joyce and William Butler Yeats, must in her search for meaning create her own rituals.

At any rate ritualistic riddles become plausible for Dickinson when we look at the purposes of ritual, whatever its nature. Susanne Langer has found ritual used chiefly as a means of enjoying the drama of life, of regaining votive symbols or of articulating a relation with both nature and society.[6] And a final factor in the creation of rituals provides another rea-

[4] Marshall Van Deusen, "Dickinson's 'Further in Summer Than the Birds,'" *The Explicator* 13 (March, 1955): Item 33.

[5] Porter, *The Art of Emily Dickinson's Early Poetry*, pp. 138–139.

[6] Susanne Langer, *Philosophy in a New Key* (Cambridge: Harvard University Press, 1960), pp. 155–160.

son why a ritual may also be a riddle, other than the fact that the subject is less likely to be understood or experienced by contemporary man. Again Susanne Langer, in noting the formal and cursory qualities of the ritual, wrote, almost, it might seem, with Emily Dickinson in mind: "It [the ritual] becomes an act of *reference* rather than of representation."[7] Just as Emily Dickinson seems to have written riddles to increase her privacy by "omitting the center," deleting the circumstance of a poem too well-known to be repeated to her audience, so she created rituals which repeatedly capture and make formal the drama of life, not by representing it but by omitting the center, by circuiting the obvious; in short, by telling it "slant" to the initiates.

Finally, whether Emily Dickinson is an exponent of *Angst*, or, as is the burden of this study, a proponent of a form rooted firmly in earliest oral and written traditions; whether she is ancient or modern, theirs or ours, Millicent Todd Bingham's assessment of her is in one sense both penetrating and bracing to all students of Emily Dickinson. She wrote:

Indeed, I have at times suspected that what we think of Emily's poetry is more a measure of ourselves than of her. By our changing attitudes toward it we can estimate our own growth . . . .[8]

[7] *Ibid.*, p. 156.
[8] Millicent Todd Bingham, *Ancestor's Brocades* (New York: Harper & Brothers, 1945), p. 100.

[137]

But such a conclusion, by focusing attention on the individual's subjective response to Emily Dickinson, obviously ignores the poet's creative problem and avoids many of the critical problems as well. It must surely be apparent that before we can make her "ours" she must first be "theirs"; before we can claim her for our own, we must find her place in a generation which did not permit her, without the ambiguity of the riddle, to "tell all the truth." Compelled to the close of her life to "tell all the truth/ but tell it slant," she early learned that "success in circuit lies."

ACKNOWLEDGEMENTS

Selected passages from Emily Dickinson's work are reprinted by permission of the publishers and the Trustees of Amherst College from Thomas H. Johnson, editor, The Poems of Emily Dickinson *and Thomas H. Johnson and Theodora V. W. Ward, editors,* The Letters of Emily Dickinson, *Cambridge, Mass.: The Belknap Press of Harvard University Press, Copyright 1955, 1958, and by the President and Fellows of Harvard College.*

By permission of Little, Brown and Co., from The Complete Poems of Emily Dickinson *by Thomas H. Johnson, editor, the following poems are reprinted in whole or in part: numbers 341, 754, 906, Copyright 1929, © 1957 by Mary L. Hampson; numbers 369, 391, 531, 905, Copyright 1935 by Martha Dickinson Bianchi, © 1963 by Mary L. Hampson; numbers 9, 14, 61, 153, 985, 1295, Copyright 1914, 1942 by Martha Dickinson Bianchi.*

Passages from numbers 8 and 12 are reprinted from The Life and Letters of Emily Dickinson, *by Martha Dickinson Bianchi, Copyright 1924, by permission of Houghton Mifflin Company.*

[139]

LIST OF WORKS CONSULTED

Åhnebrink, Lars. *The Beginnings of Naturalism in American Fiction.* New York: Russell & Russell, 1961.

Aiken, Conrad. "Emily Dickinson." *The Dial* 76 (1924): 301–308.

Aldrich, Thomas Bailey. "*In Re* Emily Dickinson." *The Atlantic Monthly* 69 (January, 1892): 143.

Anderson, Charles R. *Emily Dickinson's Poetry: Stairway of Surprise.* New York: Holt, Rinehart & Winston, 1960.

Baum, Paull F., trans. *The Anglo-Saxon Riddles of the Exeter Book.* Durham, N.C.: Duke University Press, 1963.

Bingham, Millicent Todd. *Ancestor's Brocades: The Literary Debut of Emily Dickinson.* New York: Harper & Brothers, 1945.

————. *Emily Dickinson's Home: Letters of Edward Dickinson and his Family.* New York: Harper & Brothers, 1955.

Canby, H. S. *Turn West, Turn East.* Boston: Houghton Mifflin Co., 1951.

Capps, Jack L. *Emily Dickinson's Reading.* Cambridge: Harvard University Press, 1966.

Chadwick, H. M. *The Growth of Literature.* 3 vols. Cambridge, Eng. & New York: The Macmillan Co., 1940.

Chase, Richard. *Emily Dickinson.* American Men of Literature Series. New York: William Sloane Assoc., 1951.

Dupee, F. W., ed. *The Question of Henry James.* New York: Henry Holt & Co., 1945.

Ford, Thomas W. *Heaven Beguiles the Tired.* University, Alabama: University of Alabama Press, 1966.

Gelpi, Albert J. *Emily Dickinson: The Mind of the Poet.* Cambridge: Harvard University Press, 1965.

Georges, Robert A. and Dundes, Alan. "Toward a Structural Definition of the Riddle." *Journal of American Folklore* 76 (1963): 111–118.

Griffith, Clark. *The Long Shadow: Emily Dickinson's Tragic Poetry.* New Jersey: Princeton University Press, 1964.

Higgins, David. *Portrait of Emily Dickinson: The Poet and Her Prose.* Brunswick, New Jersey: Rutgers University Press, 1964.

Higginson, T. W. and Todd, Mabel Loomis, eds. *Poems by Emily Dickinson.* Introduction by T. W. Higginson. Boston: Roberts Brothers, 1890.

Hogue, Caroline. "Dickinson's 'I Heard a Fly Buzz When I Died.'" *The Explicator* 20 (1961): Item 26.

Jenkins, MacGregor. *Emily Dickinson: Friend and Neighbor.* Boston: Little, Brown and Co., 1930.

Johnson, Thomas H., ed. *The Poems of Emily Dickin-*

son. 3 vols. Cambridge: The Belknap Press of Harvard University Press, 1955.

———. *Emily Dickinson: An Interpretative Biography.* Cambridge: Harvard University Press, 1955.

——— and Ward, Theodora, eds. *The Letters of Emily Dickinson.* 3 vols. Cambridge: The Belknap Press of Harvard University Press, 1958.

Krook, Dorothea. *The Ordeal of Consciousness in Henry James.* New York: Cambridge University Press, 1962.

Langer, Susanne. *Philosophy in a New Key.* Cambridge: Harvard University Press, 1960.

Leyda, Jay. *The Years and Hours of Emily Dickinson.* 2 vols. New Haven: Yale University Press, 1960.

MacLeish, Archibald. *Poetry and Experience.* Boston: Houghton Mifflin Co., 1961.

Matthiessen, F. O. *Henry James: The Major Phase.* New York: Oxford University Press, 1960.

Merriam, George S. *The Life and Times of Samuel Bowles.* 2 vols. New York: Century, 1885.

Porter, David. *The Art of Emily Dickinson's Early Poetry.* Cambridge: Harvard University Press, 1966.

Rapin, René. "Dickinson's 'Further in Summer than the Birds.'" *The Explicator* 12 (1954): Item 24.

Rourke, Constance. *American Humor: A Study of the National Character.* New York: Harcourt Brace & Co., 1931.

Schlauch, Margaret. *The Gift of Tongues.* New York: Dover, 1955.

Sebeok, Thomas A., ed. *Myth: A Symposium.* Bloomington: University of Indiana Press, 1958.

Sewall, Richard B. *The Lyman Letters: New Light on*

Emily Dickinson and Her Family. Amherst: University of Massachusetts Press, 1963.

Smith, Grover. "Dickinson's 'A Route of Evanescence.' " *The Explicator* 7 (1949): Item 54.

Spiller, Robert; Thorp, Willard; Johnson, Thomas H.; Canby, Henry S.; and Ludwig, Richard M., eds. *Literary History of the United States.* New York: Macmillan, 1963.

Tate, Allen. "Emily Dickinson." *The Symposium* 3 (1932): 206–226.

Taylor, Archer O. *English Riddles from Oral Tradition.* Berkeley: University of California Press, 1951.

———, "Riddles Dealing with Family Relationships." *Journal of American Folklore* 51 (1938): 25–37.

Thackrey, Donald E. *Emily Dickinson's Approach to Poetry.* Lincoln, Neb.: University of Nebraska Studies, 1954.

Twain, Mark. *Pudd'nhead Wilson.* 1894. Reprint. New York: New American Library, 1964.

Van Deusen, Marshall. "Dickinson's 'Further in Summer than the Birds.' " *The Explicator* 13 (1955): Item 33.

Whicher, George F. *This Was a Poet.* New York: Charles Scribner's Sons, 1938.

Williams, Margaret, ed. and trans. *The Word Hoard.* New York: Sheed and Ward, 1940.

Winters, Yvor. *In Defense of Reason.* Denver: Alan Swallow, 1947.

Wright, Nathalia. "Emily Dickinson's Boanerges and Thoreau's Atropos: Locomotives on the Same Line?" *MLN* 72 (1957): 101–103.

Index of First Lines

General Index

ambiguity, 8, 12, 13, 26, 36, 58, 59, 72, 96, 119, 124, 132, 138
Anderson, Charles R., 3, 13, 37, 51, 55, 56, 65, 68, 99, 115
audience, 20, 26, 29, 30, 58, 59, 79–92, 106–112, 116, 119, 133

Baum, Paull F., 12, 59, 132
Bingham, Millicent Todd, 137
Bowles, Samuel, 47, 92
Bradford, Governor William, 42
Browne, Sir Thomas, 132

Calvinism, 45, 46
Canby, Henry Seidel, 93
Capps, Jack L., 6
Chadwick, H. M., 56, 57, 79
Child-roles, 21–23, 34, 36, 39, 41, 43, 48, 83
Conway, Hugh, 102
Crane, Stephen, 45

Darwin, Charles, 45, 98
Dickinson: Austin, 27, 29, 30, 32, 54, 73, 94; Edward, 22, 30, 31, 32; Gilbert, 54; Lavinia, 26, 32, 86, 94; Susan Gilbert, 18, 27, 29
death, 49, 50, 54–60, 62, 71, 72, 75, 76, 126, 127, 129; death-watch, 53, 63; personified, 69

Emerson, R. W., 37, 38, 39, 43
Exeter Book, 12, 80

Patterson, Rebecca, 5
Porter, David, 136
Puritanism, 46, 57, 62

Ransom, John Crowe, 115
riddle; ambiguity, 14, 36, 59; Anglo-Saxon, 81; death, 49, 57, 60, 66, 103, 120; Dickinson's discussion of, 17, 19, 95; Dickinson's use of, 17, 56, 79, 101, 117, 122, 131, 132, 134, 135; elements of, 9, 12, 132; family, 28, 33; German, 18; home, 24, 25; house, 75; intellectual challenge, 37, 56, 95, 112; language revitalization in, 66, 78; "life-clock," 18, 76; literary, 10, 11, 72, 75, 80, 132; literary genre, 9, 131; major device in Dickinson's work, 6, 14, 95; metaphorical, 14; nature, 34, 35, 36; neck-riddle, 134; Nordic, 14–15fn; philosophical, 61, 62, 77, 78, 134; physiological, 62, 65, 67, 77, 78, 134; psychological, 60, 77, 78, 134; religious dilemma expressed in, 45, 47, 48, 49; riddle of death, 55, 60, 76, 82, 110, 120, 126; riddle poems, 33, 95, 108; used for satire, 44; used for anonymity, 23, 137
ritual, 136, 137
Root, Abiah, 52
Rourke, Constance, 22

society, 41

Tate, Allen, 8, 46
Taylor, Archer, 75
Thackrey, Donald, 79, 118
Thoreau, Henry David, 39, 40, 44
Todd, Mabel Loomis, 91, 93, 94, 95, 96
transcendentalism, 62
Twain, Mark, 41, 53, 63

Van Deusen, Marshall, 136

Whicher, George, 50, 107
Whitman, Walt, 39, 40, 44

A Note on the Type

The text of this book was set on the Linotype in a face called Monticello. This type, issued by Mergenthaler Linotype in 1950, is based on a cutting called "Ronaldson Roman No. 1," a late eighteenth-century production of the Binny & Ronaldson foundry, Philadelphia, Pa. *Monticello* belongs to the family of transitional faces which includes *Bell Roman, Baskerville, Bulmer* and *Fournier*. The Transitionals fall between the hearty Old Style taste represented by Caslon's letters, and the stylization of nineteenth-century Moderns.

The Indian Pipes design stamped in gold on the front board was used on the first edition of Emily Dickinson's poems.

The paper is Warrens Old Style Laid, the cloth, Riverside Chambray.

The book was printed and bound by the Kingsport Press, Inc., Kingsport, Tenn. The internal typographic design is by Guy Fleming. The binding design is by the publisher.

[151]